SMART MOVES

SMART MOVES

HOW TO SUCCEED IN SCHOOL, SPORTS, CAREER, AND LIFE

Dick DeVenzio

Prometheus Books

59 John Glenn Drive
Amherst, New York 14228-2197

Inquiries should be addressed to
Prometheus Books
59 John Glenn Drive
Amherst, New York 14228–2197
VOICE: 716–691–0133, ext. 207
FAX: 716–564–2711
WWW.PROMETHEUSBOOKS.COM

Library of Congress Cataloging-in-Publication Data

DeVenzio, Richard, 1949–
   Smart moves.
      Summary: Offers advice to young adults on how they can achieve goals by developing a positive attitude and the appropriate drive to succeed. Suggests various study strategies and self-promotion plans.
      1. Youth—United States—Life skills guides—Juvenile literature. 2. Young adults—United States—Life skills guides—Juvenile literature. 3. Attitude change—Juvenile literature.4. Self-actualization (Psychology)—Juvenile literature. [1. Life skills. 2. Self-actualization] I. Title.

HQ796.D425   1989   305.23'5'0973   89–10541
ISBN 0–87975–546–6

Printed in the United States of America on acid-free paper

Table of Contents

Get Fired Up!

Why do some people attack each day and use their abilities to the fullest, while many others trudge through life just getting by? Why isn't everyone able to fire on all cylinders, to work, play, and study in *peak* condition?

Are you motivated to be the best person you can be—or are you skeptical about the very word "motivation"? You may worry that a so-called motivator will try to get you to do things your parents or teachers want you to do, but not what you want for yourself.

Please let me shatter that concept from the start. I don't have any interest in getting you to do the things your parents or teachers want. In fact, I happen to think that the world is suffering from a shortage of people who are willing to strike out on their own, think their own thoughts, ask their own questions, make their own decisions, and draw their own conclusions.

My reason for writing this book is to help you unlock your own personal power *for whatever you want to do.* What you do with it is up to you. Dropping out or rebelling is fine—as long as it is done energetically. But don't waste your life putting in listless time, just getting by.

Parents, teachers, and other authority figures may be queasy about encouraging you to search for your own spiritual and moral values and your own ideas, and they may be downright angry about my willingness to encourage your rebellion. But I don't care. I don't think the world is in such outstanding condition that any parents, teachers, or authority figures can argue for perpetuating things as they are. Through this book, I hope that I can encourage you to strike out on your own, to identify your own frontiers, and to find uses for your special talents and ways of living that satisfy *you*.

> *A successful person is not*
> *one who has found the right set of*
> *circumstances,*
> *but rather, one who has developed the right set of*
> *attitudes.*

If this book has one major premise it is this: with the right attitude you can confront any circumstance, achieve any goal, or deal with any failure or setback. Attitude is indeed everything. Yet having "the right attitude" is more than just talking about a good attitude, or saying that you want to have a good attitude. It takes thought and effort and time to develop what I like to call "an unassailable action attitude," which prepares you to deal with nearly all situations with confidence, pride, and assurance.

The first section of this book is about developing an unassailable action attitude. Other sections cover a wide range of topics, including getting along with the opposite sex, easy ways of studying and being successful in school, and using hypnosis for success in sports, dieting, and forming habits. Naturally, I hope that you will be able to get some useful information and ideas from each of these sections, but I consider the first to be the most important because, truly, if you can develop the right set of attitudes, everything else in life will fall in line.

Good luck.

1

Building an
Unassailable Action Attitude

Too many players go into games holding some superficial, positive, middle-class, you-can-do-it picture in their minds while some mean, determined SOB just jams the ball down their dainty little throats. . . .

Roll into the Crack

Someone has given you this book and said, "It'll help you." And you may have thought, Oh no. The kiss of death. Not another attempt to help.

Many of you are tired of getting help. You just want to be left alone to do your own thing, find your own way.

I understand. They sent you to school; they took you to the dentist; they made you swallow some terrible thick syrup. All because "it'll help you. It's good for you."

Okay. So *they* are wrong sometimes. They don't know everything. But don't think that everything they say is stupid just because you have disagreed with *some* things. Don't get so rebellious that you just reject everything they throw at you.

Make your own decisions. *You* decide what's what. If something is good for you, use it. If it isn't, reject it. But give everything a chance. That goes for this book, too.

If you think this book is going to "cheer" you toward some adult's idea of success, you are wrong.

I'm not much into cheerleadering myself. You know: "Hey, rah-rah. Fight, team, fight. You can do it. Think positive."

This kind of talk doesn't impress me, either. First of all, "positive" is an adverb. (If you're gonna think at all, it has to be "positive*ly*."

Think positively. That's better. But I still don't like it.)

I believe in thinking negatively. Going into a big game, for example, I believe you should think about losing.

"Losing?" you might say. "Oh no. Don't say that. Don't mention it. Think positively. Think about winning. You can do it. Imagine yourself winning. Hold it in your mind. You can do it. You can do it."

I hear that kind of chatter a lot, but I don't like it. I like realism: "We could *lose*. We could get our butts whipped." You get the picture?

Too many players go into games holding some superficial, positive, middle-class, you-can-do-it picture in their minds while some mean, determined SOB just jams the ball down their dainty little throats, because he hates losing and can't stand to think about walking off the field having lost to *them*. He has a clear picture of losing. He has lost before. He has watched other people accept trophies and get interviewed. And he has seen them gloat and talk big and act cool—and it makes him sick.

He holds a picture of defeat in his mind and it propels him. It enables him to play with desperation and urgency and effort. And he never walks off a field wondering what went wrong and why he didn't try harder, because he tried as hard as he could the whole time, trying to avoid the feelings and pictures of failure.

You can do it? Maybe it's better to think of what it's like to fail. That way you will get off your butt and work and do something. Forget all this picture crap. *Do* something. Work. Go after it. Drive yourself. Put your abilities into the fray. When you're knocked down, get back up. Work. Fight. Use your energy. It's there for you to utilize. Why save it?

You can do anything you set your mind to, right?

Hell no!

This book isn't going to perpetrate those typical self-help-book myths. Some of you thin little creeps reading this want to be linebackers for the Pittsburgh Steelers. Forget it. You ain't gonna do that. You're too small and it's too late. Some of you tall willowy girls want be be champion gymnasts. Sorry. You can't.

A lot of things you cannot do, regardless of whether you set your mind to them or not.

Forget all this "you can do it" garbage, and start being realistic.

Dream, yes. But *think,* too. What is possible? What is not possible? How can you know one from the other?

Make some progress. Too many people spend their whole lives mapping out journeys and wondering if they can climb this or that mountain, when they haven't even gotten over the first hill yet.

Get over the first hill, *then* decide about the second.

So you want to get out of where you are and be rich and famous and live in a mansion and boss a thousand people around and have millions of fans writing you letters, drawing your picture, and kissing your ring? Fine. But don't sit around *thinking* about it. Start *doing* something about it. Climb the first hill. Take a small step. Get out of the cabin and onto the trail. Move toward your vision.

Don't stand at a distance and try to make out what's going on up ahead. It's too blurry from this far back. Get closer, where you can see what the hell is going on up there!

I'm sorry for using this "bad" language, but I think it is a lot worse to speak in nice sociological, textbook terms that put you to sleep and let you keep living a stupid life. If it takes some bad words to wake you up, I'm not afraid of that. I'll chance it, even at the risk of losing a few fragile folks along the way.

What's my point? This is *not* the same old you-can-do-it motivation book. It's a book that can help you to think clearly about what you are doing with your life, about how you can learn to use and build your power.

We all have within us a kernel of power—the ability to explode, you might say. Think of an acorn. Inside that acorn is "nothing." Some sticky stuff. You can take the shell off an acorn, and put it under a microscope, and there is still nothing in there that gives any hint at all of a giant oak tree standing in the midst of a powerful storm—strong, mighty, undaunted.

That powerful mighty oak tree came from an acorn, from that sticky nothing inside the tiny little shell lying there on the ground.

Mighty oaks from tiny acorns grow.

It's true. Just like great people, rich people, famous people, presidents, kings, athletes, and movie stars all come from little kids, babies who can't talk, can't walk, can't feed themselves, can't even sit up on their own.

There's no secret. No magic. Just some common sense, some

logical steps to take in order to go from acorn to oak tree, from little kid to rich guy, or baby to movie star.

Before you set out on your journey, it makes sense to know some of the steps. After all, a lot of acorns have failed to become oak trees. A lot of little kids have grown up stupid and discouraged.

Why not grow up smart and active? Active-for-what is for *you* to decide. You do what you want with your life. But whatever you do, you ought to know how to develop your personal power. You ought to give yourself the opportunity to rise from the ground and stand strong, powerful, and undaunted in the face of storms that knock others down and out. Why not?

Why not?

You have a choice. Stay on the cement where there's no soil, no water, no chance to grow. Or roll over into the crack, into the dirt. Sink some roots, drink some rain, and bust through the cement, crack the sidewalk, take over the place, rise to the sky, and command the area.

It's up to you—and it just takes a tiny step forward. This book can show you how.

Packs of hyenas howling a few yards away, wolves growling,
huge birds flapping their wings and waiting impatiently for the leftovers.
Do you think the lion hurries?

Living Between Your Own Ears

If there is one crucial concept that is important to living well, it is learning to live between your own ears.

It doesn't sound like much at first. You think everyone does it. But on further consideration, you will realize that most people don't live between their ears; they live "out there" in the air, like a tiny tree in the middle of a field, buffeted constantly by the winds of conversations and orders and instructions.

Think about it. You wake up. You are feeling fine. It promises to be a good day. Then you hear somebody say something bad about you—and your day suddenly changes. You are upset, angry, on edge.

Everything has changed because of something that happened outside of your ears, not between them. You let those comments reach you and mar your day. It was not inevitable. It was not necessary. You *let* it happen. You chose to live outside your ears, instead of between them.

Lions and Sparrows

Think of the difference between lions and sparrows, the way they go about life and where they live.

A sparrow can see its absolute favorite meal on the ground,

and what does it do? It looks around, it flies near. A big fat juicy worm. The best brand. It begins to peck, hears something, flies off. Looks around. Flies nearby. Looks. Moves. Looks. Back and forth. A step closer. A step back. Look. What? Move. Retreat. Go near. Fly away. Come back. Peck. Move. Run. Fly back. Peck. Peck. Peck. Move. Fly away. Fly back. Peck. Retreat. Look. What? Approach. Look. Step back. Step forward. Peck.

Could *you* enjoy a meal like that? The sparrow is influenced by every tiny movement. Every breeze, shadow, and twig invades its consciousness. It jumps around, looks around, dances around, and does hundreds of things besides just sitting down to its favorite meal.

The lion on the other hand is the ultimate in living between its ears. It walks out onto a prairie with big hairy, smelly creatures everywhere. Giant hooves and tusks and horns and teeth all around. Neighing, growling, roaring, chirping, howling going on everywhere. And the lion chooses its spot, plunks down and goes to sleep. Sleeps till it's hungry. Then gets up and stretches and limbers up, and lets everyone know with a thunderous roar that it is hungry and is about to kill its dinner.

What an incredible difference in lifestyle from the sparrow. The lion kills something and eats it right there on the spot. Packs of hyenas howling a few yards away, wolves growling, huge birds flapping their wings and waiting impatiently for the leftovers. Do you think the lion hurries?

Lions always eat at the same speed. The vultures and hyenas and wolves can wait, and will wait. The lion takes its time, eats till it's full, then walks off a few feet where the air smells better and plunks down on the ground again to sleep. It's up to the others to drag the leftovers away where they can try to eat in peace.

Now think about it. Which are you? A sparrow? Or a lion? Do you live between your ears? Or "out there" in the air where the roars and howls and growls of life are a constant source of bother and worry?

It's up to you. The sparrow or the lion?

"Don't Mess with My Graph":
Your Personal Richter Scale

A Richter scale measures seismic activity, the amount of force created by earthquakes and smaller ground movements. A huge quake, one that shakes buildings and breaks windows for miles around, may register as a six on the scale. A seven might actually knock the buildings down, uproot trees, turn over cars.

The Richter scale and the seismograph, which records that seismic activity, are useful for thinking about your own life. What if we put your life on the scale? And measured your ups and downs as though they were seismic activity on the graph?

What would your graph look like?

A huge quake sends the needle up, way up near the top of the graph. When the force is gone, the needle drops back down. So what moves your needle? What makes you happy and excited and gets you "high"? And what makes you unhappy, discouraged, and gets you down?

Once you begin thinking of your life as a graph, it can change your whole way of doing things. Suddenly it makes perfect sense to avoid negative people.

"Hey, man, you're trying to pull down my graph. Sorry, no thank you. I'm not interested."

It makes sense to try to live on a high plane, near the top of the graph, to seek out people, events, and opportunities that keep the needle up. Just as it makes sense to avoid negative people, extricate yourself from negative situations and rise above them.

When you really begin to think about graphing your life, you become like a security guard, protecting your graph. You want that needle—your life—to stay high, and you are willing to work to keep it there. Now argumentative people can be seen for exactly what they are: people who are trying to bring you down, pull down your graph, make you live at a lower level.

Don't do it! Don't let 'em mess with your graph. Guard your graph. Protect it. That's your job. That's your life.

In sports, referees, coaches, teammates, opposing players, fans— everyone—will try to lower your graph. But you don't have to let them. You can live above it all.

In school, teachers, principals, and other students will all try to lower your graph. But don't let them. You can live above it all, between your own ears, high on the scale.

At home you will get orders, perhaps unreasonable demands. You may just want to get out, but you can't. You live there. You are right there in the midst of it all. There is no escape.

Hold it. There is always an escape. No one lives between your ears but you. They can talk to you, bark at you, order you to do this or that. But they cannot control what you think. They cannot keep you from imagining a better life. They cannot keep you from concentrating on future plans, on what you will be doing tomorrow, next week, or next year.

Many people can assault your graph. But you have the power to protect it. You have the power to live constantly on a high plane. It's up to you. You merely have to realize that your task in life is not to win every argument, not to inject your opinion into every discussion, not to comment on every situation, not to enter every fight and fray.

Your task is to protect your graph, to get your needle up—and keep it up. Do the things, be in the places, see the people who get your graph up. Avoid as much as possible the things and places and people that bring your graph down.

Graphing Your Life

To help you understand even better exactly what moves *your* needle up and down, consider making a couple of graphs of your own life. First, try a "Life Graph," marking all the best highs and the worst lows. For me, the lows would be wetting my pants in kindergarten, getting beat up by a big kid (a second grader when I was in first grade), getting paddled in seventh grade in front of the whole class, not being elected captain of my Little League team, losing a big game my junior year in high school, losing my date at the junior prom (a bad year!), getting a new coach in college (one I disliked), and watching my mother slowly die of cancer. Those are the lows of my life.

The highs would include being selected by my kindergarten class to deliver a basket of fruit to an orphanage—and getting to sit with Paula Matisz, the girl who was selected; making the Little League team as a nine-year-old; pitching my team to the town championship when I was eleven; making the junior high team in seventh grade; my first kiss, with Gayle Godfrey; winning a state championship in basketball; completing my first book; getting a job in the Caribbean; making love with an absolutely exquisite woman; and putting together a successful Sports Foundation convention.

Do a graph like this for yourself, from birth to the present. Think of all the lows, and all the highs, and mark them down. What floats *your* boat?

The graph will reveal things about yourself you may not have known. It may help you to decide what to strive for and how to spend your life. What was your most recent high point? When do you expect your next one? What are you doing to get to the next special high point?

In the same way, look at the lows. How can you avoid future lows? How can you smooth them out? Obviously you cannot do anything about the death of someone you love. But you can do something about your response to it. You can learn that no one can live forever, that you have to enjoy life while you can, enjoy your friends and your family while you have them. Do your best now to appreciate what you have, so that when it's gone—or when they are gone—at least you will not experience regret. You will know that you did what you could when you could.

A Daily Graph

To bring your life into focus on a daily basis, you should consider graphing a day in your life, just the way you graphed your entire life. What things during a typical day make you the most high? What things bring you down? When you see these things on paper in front of you, it makes it a lot easier to see your life clearly and to multiply the highs while avoiding or at least reducing the lows.

Do you grumble through the mornings, having brainwashed yourself over a period of time by telling yourself you are not "a morning person"? Have you ever stopped to think about your morning behavior with a clear perspective? What are you like typically? What would you be like on a morning when you were scheduled to receive a million dollars at 10:00 A.M., provided you were not late?

Obviously, *not* being a morning person is merely a result of having had the luxury over a period of time of acting like a jerk and getting away with it. If there had been some rewards along the way for acting excited and enthusiastic in the mornings—lo and behold—you would be a morning person, in the habit of waking up excited to meet the new day and enthusiastic about life.

What gets you up? What brings you down? Graph a few days in a row, then go through the days thinking about where you are on the graph. Is your lunch break your high for the day? Is work a drag? Do you live for coffee breaks and lunch breaks? If so, you need to get another job!

If you dislike school so much that your highs happen each day when the bells ring to end each class—and your lows are the classes themselves—you need to quit school, or take time to find out why some people like it, and how you possibly can too.

Your graph will tell you a story, one that you need to act on. Because it is foolish to spend your life in the depths, at the low end of your graph. Life is too short. Life is too precious. Maybe it's time for you take, among other things, the water test.

It doesn't have to be fresh clean mountain air
or air from an ocean breeze.
Sooty, polluted air will do just fine for the moment.

The Water Test

The world is filled with complainers who have lots of excuses.

There are always dozens of "legitimate" reasons why you didn't do this or didn't do that, why you would've, could've, should've.

But when all is said and done, the excuses are not worth the paper they're printed on. What were the results? Forget about the reasons why you did or did not do something. What *did* you do? That's what life comes down to. We already know that it rains sometimes, that the conditions are not always ideal, that so-and-so can be counted on to say such-and-such, and that thousands of reasons can be given for your moods, your inactions, your foolish decisions, your failures.

The water test can put all this into perspective for you—every day when you wake up. Try it. It only takes a minute or two.

Go to your sink, cover the drain, and fill the sink with water. Then put your head in the water.

Presto! You've done it.

Do you know what the answer to all of your problems is? Just one thing. Hold your head under thirty seconds, a minute, longer. Just wait. It will become very clear to you, very soon, that the only thing that *really* matters to you is pulling your head up and breathing. Taking a nice big gulp of air. It doesn't have to fresh clean mountain air or air from an ocean breeze. Sooty, polluted air will do just fine for the moment. Understand?

If you don't, you need to try it. Once you have, once you really think about it, you'll have little regard for people's excuses for their so-called moods.

"Oh, so you're not a morning person? You just can't seem to get going in the morning? You just can't seem to get yourself dressed up to go job hunting? You just can't seem to stay awake in class? Hey, I understand—how 'bout walking over to the sink here with me and let me help you think more clearly. Put your head under . . . yeah . . . and wave your hand when you're about to come up . . . and I'll do you the favor of holding your head down a couple of minutes longer . . . just a couple of minutes . . . and you won't have a worry, a desire, or an excuse in the world. All you will care about is breathing."

The Famed Hospital Walk

From time to time, some movie star or celebrity can be seen on television talking about visiting a hospital and being so touched by what he or she saw: Little kids struggling to take one step. Old people gasping for breath. Soldiers missing limbs. Teenagers with burns.

Big deal. What did they expect? Are *you* so narrow-minded that you have to walk through a hospital to understand that people are getting burned and shot and cut and crippled? If you need to walk through a hospital to understand how lucky you are to have your set of problems and worries, then do it. Walk in. Look around. If you haven't thought about it, think about it. Maybe the movie star is right to tell that story. Maybe people do need to be reminded.

But maybe you should just remind yourself every day with the water test, every day, until it is no longer in the back of your mind but in the front. Remind yourself that you are lucky to have your struggles, and that, if your circumstances were changed only slightly, you would gladly ask for the set of problems you have now and agree to attack them with enthusiasm.

Disagree? Is it truly so hard to stay awake in that one boring class? How about a quick choice? Let's walk over to the sink first.

Good. Put your head in. You'll make your choice in two minutes.

Stay under, or commit yourself to enthusiasm in that class? You'll choose the latter. But how will you do it? Six big law-enforcement officers are not going to follow you to class and watch you. If you are not truly excited to be there, find some ways to *pretend*. That will do for starters. It's up to you. There's a sink just outside class.

You may be thinking this is crazy, this whole sink thing with the police. But guess what? There are literally millions of people on this earth who do understand, who are grateful for the short, precious life they have, and who are trying to maximize every moment for just that reason. They don't expect everything to be perfect. They don't expect a path through life free of obstacles. They are simply happy to be breathing and walking effortlessly, and therefore they are living life to the best of their ability.

Did you get that? Millions. Literally millions. If you are dragging through your life on a low plane of existence, resorting to excuses to justify your laziness, moodiness, and failures, then you don't really understand life yet.

Walking and breathing effortlessly. If you are doing those things, you are doing things that many people cannot.

Now what? You don't look like a beauty queen or movie star? You are not as strong as an Olympic weight-lifter? You are not as graceful as a prima ballerina? Not as coordinated as a tennis star? Not as smart as the valedictorian at Harvard?

Big deal. So your parents are out to lunch. Your teachers are boring. Your coach is an idiot. You're out of work and out of money.

Big deal.

Put your head under the water and think about it. Wait under there until you've thought carefully. Wait till you're desperate. Wait till you are begging for air. Then go out and grab your problems and your opportunities by the throat and squeeze. No other approach makes any sense, unless you're so narrow-minded that you still think the world owes you a magic-carpet ride through life. Do you really need to be left with some inspiring words?

A wolf can howl all night but the moon doesn't care!

*What do I care if "C-squared equals A-squared plus B-squared"?
Or, what do I care if the squaw on the hippopotamus
is equal to "some" of the squaws on the other two hides?*

The Squaw on the Hippopotamus

Education and "I'll never need this stuff"

One of the most common misconceptions that leads students astray, or helps them to feel justified in not giving their best in a classroom, is the question, "When will I ever use *this?*" or the confident assertion, "I'll never need *that*. What do I care if C-squared equals A-squared plus B-squared?" Or, as it was once said, "What do I care if the squaw on the hippopotamus is equal to 'some' of the squaws on the other two hides?"

Of course, those questions can be applied to just about anything: Why do I need to know about Vasco da Gama sailing around the tip of Africa? That already happened. What good is a foreign language to me? I'm staying in America. Why do I need to know how to diagram a sentence? I can already talk.

If your litmus test or measuring stick for education is "when-will-I-need-it?" you may very well be able to justify never doing anything at all—except learning one task that will enable you to do one manual job. For example, if you plan to work on an assembly line, you need to learn to take something off a shelf and put it on a conveyor belt. You'll do that over and over, thousands of times, perhaps millions of times over the course of a lifetime. Delivering papers would come under that category; so would garbage collecting and stocking shelves.

By the time you do those kinds of jobs for a few years, you may discover that machines or robots will be replacing you—because they can do the same tasks over and over, day after day, with fewer errors (and probably more enthusiasm) than most humans. Another problem is that jobs that require the same manual effort over and over again rarely pay very much, since anyone—including a machine—can be easily taught to do them.

High-paying jobs, on the other hand, cannot be taught in a day—because there is not any one particular thing you have to do over and over again. Instead, your job is to solve new problems each day: to figure out how to make your workers perform more efficiently, how to streamline your operations, how to organize a wide variety of tasks, how to help people work together in order to be more productive.

Problems like these can't be taught in a day. Often they can't even be anticipated. They just come up, in new ways all the time. Neither a chimpanzee nor a robot can help two tense people iron out a difference of opinion and begin working together. It takes a person with a brain, someone who can hear two conflicting ideas that cover a large set of problems and procedures, to arrive at a solution that both people not only can accept but can commit themselves to and work toward.

That's where the "hippopotamus" of the right triangle comes in. And you thought you'd never need it!

The only way you can be in a position to solve a complex problem that has never before arisen is by having a mind that is well exercised. If your mind confronts the new problem having already solved dozens, maybe hundreds or thousands of other problems, then it just may be able to solve the new problem. You take a little bit of knowledge from one problem and a bit from another and another, and things begin to fit together. New ideas suggest themselves as a *synthesis* of various solutions to other past problems.

If that sounds complicated, *it is!* That's precisely why education is complicated, precisely why you spend time in school learning things and solving problems that you claim you will never need again. Think about it. If you were faced with trying to solve a territorial dispute between Israel and the Palestinian Liberation Organization, would you want to send someone who had spent his or her whole life putting a nut on a screw, or would you send someone who had mastered geometry and Latin and biology and music? You could ask, "What good will triangles and strange words and dissected frogs and G-clefs do someone who is trying to solve a territorial dispute?" The answer of course is *experience in solving problems,* experience in understanding patterns and relationships. Perhaps the harmonies of music, triangles, or language may suggest a solution to a different kind of problem.

Of course, problems in the real world are complex. It takes a well-exercised brain to deal with them and to come up with solutions that have a chance to work.

If you think of the brain as a muscle, it becomes apparent that the only way to prepare it for a race or contest is to exercise it, stretch it this way and that. An athlete cannot anticipate what kind of cuts, turns, leaps, or acrobatic moves may be necessary during the course of a game or competition. Therefore, preparation must include drills, exercises, and training that prepares the muscles to do whatever is called for at the moment.

Once you begin to fully understand that the brain is a kind of muscle, you'll never again ask the question, "When will I ever need this or that?" In fact, *everything* will suddenly make sense—as much sense as more push-ups, toe touches, back stretches, sit-ups, and other warm-ups, as well as planning what to do when your competitor "throws you a curve."

To prepare adequately to win an athletic competition, you need to go over all sorts of possibilities. Those who coach team sports must give each player assignments for every likely situation. Yet even the great coaches can't anticipate everything that will come up, so they train reactions and thinking and concepts, preparing their teams to make good decisions accordingly.

To do a complex job well, creatively, intelligently, or to put together an innovative plan that opens up a whole new market may indeed take everything you have ever been exposed to. Wade Boggs didn't line the first knuckleball he ever saw into left field. He missed it—and he may never have figured out how to hit a knuckler had he not already seen thousands of curves, sliders, and split-fingered fastballs.

Put in proper perspective, you will never again have to wonder why you are studying this or that, or what good it will do you, or when you will ever use it. Everything you ever learn will be used every day!

The definition of education now comes clearly into focus. *Education is a series of seemingly meaningless challenges that prepare you for an unknowable future.*

Taken individually, no particular thing you learn or are forced to study may seem to have any bearing on your later life. Yet, taken cumulatively, each one fills in a piece of the puzzle, part of the bigger picture, part of the mozaic that will enable you to solve problems, the nature of which cannot be anticipated.

Now, why do you need a language? What a terrific way of developing a sense of grammar, of relationships, of patterns, and of meaning. There's a lot more to it than "See Dick run."

Why do you need to know that the circumference of a circle can be obtained by some crazy number called *pi*? You are learning relationships, patterns, harmony.

Languages, mathematics, history, sociology, biology, chemistry. One blends into another. All awaken the mind and exercise that muscle—enabling it to do more and more.

So, do you need calculus? Maybe not. Maybe you don't need vitamin C either. Not to live. But you may need it to run fast, or to have a high energy level, or to remain enthusiastic.

Do you *need* algebra? Why not ask if you need fruit? Do you *need* geology? Do you need potassium in your diet?

If you are just trying to get by, there are all sorts of things you don't need.

If you are trying to live your life "full steam ahead," then you not only need science and math and languages and social sciences; it also would be worthwhile to come into contact with a strict disciplinarian, or maybe a very demanding coach. Perhaps some lunatics, too. And, of course, some boring teachers.

*When mining for diamonds, you cannot expect to be
dazzled by brilliance, or you will be disappointed.
The diamonds will not be sitting there shining in the sun.
Instead, they will be encrusted in rock, dull and dirty,
waiting to be uncovered.*

Shakespeare, Opera, and Oak Trees

Response to Boredom

Perhaps the key ingredient needed for success in school—and in life itself—is an intelligent response to boredom.

Let's say it in another, more common way. In fact, let's let typical stupidity speak for itself. Consider the following exchange.

"Hey, how d'you do in English class?"

"Ah hey, man, you know that teacher in there. She must be a hundred years old. Best cure for insomnia known to modern medicine! All we did in there was diagram sentences. Gawd, is that stuff boring!"

"Yeah. What d'you get?"

"Be real. How could anyone stay awake long enough to pass that crap?"

That exchange, in slightly altered form, takes place constantly. A student flunks a course and tries to justify it by saying the teacher wasn't good. Would you take a moment to concentrate on the utter stupidity of that way of thinking?

"Hey, man, I could've played some good ball, but my coach was stupid."

"Hey, man, I could've passed that course, but the teacher was stupid."

"Hey, man, I could've had a good life, but my parents were stupid."

There are literally *millions* of people who think they can justify their own failures—all the way through life—by pointing to someone else's stupidity. *That* is the ultimate stupidity.

Blaming others for your failures must be put in perspective. Some players played well *despite* the coach. Some students passed the course despite the teacher. Some people had good lives despite their parents.

The point should be obvious. It is sheer foolishness to even mention anyone else's role in your own failure. It's *your* athletic career, *your* schoolwork—*your* life. How did you do? No one really cares about how your coaches, teachers, and parents were. Guess what? We already *know* how they were: Sometimes they were good, sometimes they were not.

No one gets perfect leadership and guidance all of the time. Some get better than others. But everyone has problems to overcome. Everyone has excuses to offer. But who cares? What difference does it make? On your report card, in the team program, in the grand Book of Life, there isn't even a place for excuses. There is no page entitled "Extenuating Reasons for Failure."

No one gives a damn about excuses. Did you succeed or did you fail? Did you pass or did you flunk? Did you play or did you get cut from the team? Did you win or did you lose?

Once you fully understand this, it may very well change your whole approach to your work and to your life. Unfortunately, you grew up making excuses for why you didn't take out the garbage, why you didn't get your room cleaned, why you didn't get your homework done. Maybe your parents accepted excuses—and gave you poor preparation for life.

So now, let's look again at the student who feels justified in flunking a course because the teacher was boring. How stupid! *Everyone* does well when the teacher is great. But how many great teachers are there in the world? How many great anythings are there? You just are not going to live your life encountering greatness everywhere. You will be lucky if you *ever* run into it. Usually, you will encounter mediocrity, perhaps competence now and then, and that's the most you can hope for. Often you will encounter incompetence. So what? It's still your life.

"But Your Honor, I would've sent in my taxes, but my accountant was bad."

"But Your Honor, I would've gotten away with the crime, but my getaway driver was bad!"

So what! No one cares about anyone else's part in your affairs. It's what *you* do that counts.

Say for instance there was a school with only exciting, entertaining teachers. You know what the principal or headmaster would have to do? *Hire some boring teachers.*

Having only exciting, entertaining teachers would be poor preparation for life. It would get you in the habit of thinking that everyone you meet for the rest of your life would be stimulating and exciting, and then you would be lost when you encountered the usual mediocrity.

In order to run a good school and prepare students for life, it is *necessary* to have boring teachers. Only boring teachers are going to be able to find out what a student is really like. If a teacher is making everyone laugh and getting everyone excited, of course everyone will pay attention and try. But what about when it is not so easy?

In athletic competition, in classrooms, and in life itself, there is a sorting-out process. The bad are weeded out. The mediocre fall behind. The challenge is to be consistent, to be committed to excellence, to be committed to a certain form of behavior, *regardless of the circumstances.*

Cracked Courts, Bad Weather, Poor Lighting . . .

In sports, coaches are accustomed to dealing with excuses, and to teaching their players that excuses have no place in the won-lost record. Left to their own thoughts, athletes will typically complain that the court was cracked, the ball had too much air or not enough, the sun was too bright, the lights were too dim, it was too hot or cold. All outstanding coaches teach their players to leave the excuses to the other team. As a result, a typical pregame "pep talk" can be expected to include something like this:

"Okay, it is very hot today. The field is in bad shape. And there is a terrific glare out there. Also, these are the worst umpires we will have all year. There will be plenty of excuses for losing today. But let's leave all of them to the other team. Let them complain about the conditions. Let them tell the reporters about the heat, the glare, and the umpires. We'll be the ones that talk about the runs we scored, about how we used the glare and the heat in our favor. Let's be the ones who explain after the game how we overcame bad conditions and went on to victory."

Three weeks after the game, no one will care much about the conditions. They will look down the list of games to see if a "W" or an "L" is there for that game. That's all that really counts. Did you win or lose? Did you try to explain your reasons for failure, or did you have the opportunity to explain what you overcame in order to succeed?

If you are going about life properly, then you understand that *there is no place in life for explanations for failure.* There is only a place for explaining how you managed to succeed.

Back to school again . . .

You have a course in Shakespeare, one in Opera, and one in Geology. All the subjects bore you. All of your teachers are terrible. Now what? Do you flunk out, and try telling the uncaring world how Shakespeare is stupid, opera sucks, and geology is useless?

Millions of people love Shakespeare. He is widely considered to be the "Master of the Ages." If you consider Shakespeare boring, perhaps the problem lies with you, not with Shakespeare. Why do you dislike what millions of others love? You may try to get away with saying, "Everyone is different." But it is not that easy. With knowledge usually comes interest and appreciation. Once you know about something, it becomes more interesting. The more educated you are, the more interested you become in a wide variety of things. People with no education at all often find just about everything boring, whereas highly educated people find almost everything interesting. That ought to tell you something.

When you make an off-hand remark like, "Opera is stupid," you need to remember that, perhaps at this very minute, thousands of people are seeking tickets to performances around the world. In New York, a huge building fills up every time Pavarotti sings. In Milan, there is an opera house called La Scala that was famous long before you were born. Year after year, old people, young people, weak people, strong people, poor people, rich people crowd into that building and stand and shout and swoon over opera singers.

It's stupid? Better think again. Before you say too much, you ought to know that people who call things stupid are usually stupid people. People who call things boring are usually boring people.

If you have a boring teacher (and certainly it is true that some teachers are more stimulating than others) it is time for you to examine yourself. What can you do to make that teacher and that subject more interesting? Look inward, not outward. That is the key. Look to yourself. Find a way to generate interest. Don't expect someone to do it for you. Good students understand this. Poor students don't.

Miss America's Class

Think for a moment, if you are a guy, what kind of student you would be in Miss America's class. Girls, what kind of student would you be in a class taught by your favorite actor? What if you were being taught what you have to do to become rich, famous, and wildly attractive to the opposite sex—and the course was guaranteed to produce the desired results? What kind of student would you be? The answer is obvious. You would be all eyes and ears, sitting in front of class, jotting notes hastily but quick to keep your eyes on the teacher so you wouldn't miss anything. You would arrive for class early, and be willing to stay late. If you weren't sure about something you would ask a question about it. You would be involved.

That is you at your best. And that is also your challenge. Why drop it just because the teacher and the subject is not quite so interesting? Why be less than your best? It really is up to you. Why not commit yourself and demand from yourself that you be constant, regardless of the class, regardless of the subject. Why should you change with each teacher and each subject?

Should you be a tiny weed in the middle of a field, blown by every passing wind? Or should you be an oak tree, strong and mighty, withstanding wind and rain and thunder and lightning—standing there unchanged? Most of us would choose to be the oak. You can choose to be the best you can be, regardless of the negative circumstances around you. There will always be negative circumstances, but why should there keep being a different you?

What if a camera were set up in each of your classes? Why should you sometimes be a model student, sometimes a poor one? Why not decide on what kind of student, what kind of person you want to be, and then be that student, be that person constantly, in every class, every day?

Consistency is what every coach looks for in an athlete. Not a player who is good one day, bad the next, good on a sunny day, bad on a rainy one. Consistency is the mark of quality—in an athlete, in a student, in a person.

The weather changes. Weak people change. But tough people are the same under all the circumstances that try to thwart their efforts. Tough people assume there will be negatives and look upon them as opportunities to rise above others. Good conditions, like exciting classes, do not sort out people or identify complainers and "excuse-mongers." But bad conditions, like boring classes and boring teachers, are excellent opportunities to demonstrate your inner quality.

From Boredom to Interest

Besides demanding consistency from yourself, do yourself a favor. When something seems boring, find out why it is interesting to others. Find out more about the subject, and have some faith along the way that most things, once you know more about them, become more interesting. The same goes for teachers. Want to turn a boring teacher into a more interesting one? Find out more about him or her. Who is he? Why does she teach? Who is in his family? What are her interests outside of class?

Almost every subject, every person, is interesting if you take the time and make the effort to let the interesting parts unfold.

When mining for diamonds, you cannot expect to be dazzled by brilliance, or you will be disappointed. The diamonds will not be sitting there shining in the sun. Instead, they will be encrusted in rock, dull and dirty, waiting to be uncovered.

Are you a passive observer, waiting to be entertained, or are you a diamond miner, on a quest to uncover and bring out the hidden beauty of the seemingly dull rocks around you? That is your challenge. There is a world of difference in those two approaches, both in schoolwork and in life.

*Live your life as though you are a card shark in a big poker game—
and you have some aces up your sleeve that you can use
anytime you get into a jam.*

The Card Up Your Sleeve

A Secret Formula for Gaining Confidence
and Getting Things Done

Anytime you have something to do, it feels good to have a method
or formula that you know you can count on—a foolproof scheme
that cannot be denied. When you have it, suddenly you have the
terrific ingredient so often talked about: confidence.

How do you get confidence? There is no secret there. You become
good at what you do. Or you get a formula you know will lead
to excellence, and then confidence just sort of seems to sneak in
on its own.

In working with young basketball players, I have often been
surprised at how often they want confidence before developing
proficiency. "Coach, I just don't have any confidence in my shot.
When I get in a game, I am afraid to shoot."

Oh, really? They *should* be afraid to shoot. If you aren't a terrific
shooter in practice, you aren't going to be a good shooter in games.
It's that simple. Practice until you can shoot ten-for-ten or nine-for-
ten each time you go to the free-throw line, and you'll suddenly find
yourself confident in game situations. If you cannot shoot that well,
you have no reason to be confident, so your fear is not merely rational,
but useful as well. Otherwise you would be trying all sorts of shots

that you couldn't make—and your whole team (to say nothing of the coach and fans) would hate you.

You cannot put the cart before the horse. You don't become confident via some mental technique and then go out and perform well. It's the other way round. You learn to perform extremely well, and then the confidence appears.

So how do you learn to perform extremely well? What is the secret formula for achieving, for getting things done?

The formula comes in three distinct parts.

1. Realize that any journey begins with a single step, and take that first step.

Regardless of what you want to do—write a book, be a star athlete, build a house, run a marathon, own a business—you have to start! Many great undertakings fail simply because they never begin at all. As a result, it makes sense to take the first step while you are still in the planning stages. If you've already started and you find that your plan requires you to take a different starting step, then take that step. Don't wait. In other words, don't be afraid to waste a step. Start three times, or eight. Keep starting. That way, when you finally get your plan finalized, you've already begun moving toward your goal.

2. Divide your journey into small steps, and commit yourself to a schedule for achieving each one. Try to take a step every day.

That is basic. It can also seem like magic, or nearly so in retrospect. Take a small step toward your goal each day. Not a huge, difficult step, but a small "takeable" step. Do something you can do, and move ahead.

Naturally, we are all impatient to achieve our goals, fulfill our dreams, realize our visions, and so on. Impatience is natural. It is a part of everyone. But it must be dealt with, understood, transformed. There isn't a whole lot more you need than to say to yourself, "I am impatient to succeed. So is everyone else. Impatience is natural. Replace it. Relax. Be patient." Say that to yourself a few times and then enjoy the towering inevitability of step 3.

3. Watch the passage of time.

If there is one thing you can count on, it is that time will pass. Try as you may, you cannot stop time from passing. That seems the same as saying nothing at all, but actually it is saying a great deal if you have followed steps 1 and 2. If you have begun, and if you have committed yourself to taking daily steps, you must go forward. If you want to write a book, writing one page a day will absolutely assure you of having a 365-page book after just one year. If you want to be a basketball player, you shoot 1000 shots every day for a year. That becomes 365,000 shots! Anyone who takes 365,000 shots becomes a good shooter. It is inevitable.

The same goes for getting stronger or thinner. Do just one push-up. Then the next day two. Each day, simply do as many as you can. There is no stopping you. At the end of the year you will be doing many push-ups, and you will be strong. There is simply no way to keep it from happening. *That* is the magic of the formula. Of course it takes effort and commitment and determination. But in some ways those are scary words—things we all fear we lack. Personally I prefer not to think in those terms. Rather, I want only to concentrate on one day. Not a full year of days. Just this day. Can I take my step today? That I can do. And I will do.

In other words, narrow your thinking. Once you decide on a course of action, forget the big picture. Deal with your challenge a day at a time. Just do today's work. Take today's tiny step, and let the inevitable passage of time work *for* you, not against you.

The Secret

Finally, there is the secret, the hidden way to getting things done and reaching your goals. The secret is in not telling anyone your plan or your steps or your goal. It's not easy! Once you have set yourself on a course, it is such a terrific temptation to share it with everyone. But don't. Sharing it is often so much fun, and gives you so much satisfaction that it removes some of the energy, some of your commitment for doing the thing.

For that reason, it is better to keep your plan to yourself. At least keep it a secret from most people. Enjoy your mystery. Live your life as though you are a card shark in a big poker game—and you have some aces up your sleeve that you can use anytime you get into a jam. You can win any hand you really want to win, because you have secret cards you can pull out.

What a feeling it is to have that kind of secret, knowing that it is just a matter of time before you put your cards on the table and win. That is exactly what you do when you put your plan into effect by starting and by taking a step a day. No one needs to know that you have set in motion a force that cannot be denied. You don't need to announce to the world that you are going to run a marathon. Just jog a bit today, and do tomorrow's jog tomorrow.

Having a secret gives life a special flavor that propels you. It is a joy to have your secret leak out, or get discovered here and there by those around you. So keep it to yourself. Trust time. It will pass. Just make sure you are filling it with your daily step. They will add up. There is no way anyone can stop you.

Think of all the cowboys and ballerinas we would have
roaming around our streets
if all the little would-be rope-masters and toe-dancers
had kept to their early desires.

Setting Goals, Making Practice Plans, and Not Being Afraid to Quit

Nearly every self-help or motivational book will talk about the importance of setting goals. Setting goals does help you to accomplish things, but goal-setting also has negative aspects that are seldom talked about. Let's discuss both sides of the coin.

First, why is goal-setting important? I once heard a speaker tell a story that illustrates the importance of setting goals:

He pointed out that nearly anyone could shoot basketball better than Larry Bird or Magic Johnson, if the pro had one simple handicap: a blindfold. Could the star shoot effectively if he couldn't see? He wouldn't even know where the basket was.

All that impressive hand-eye coordination and skill would go completely to waste if the pro didn't know where his target was. Forget the strength, the "soft touch," the fingertip control, the excellent interplay of retina and optic nerve. None of it would mean a thing if the star stood, ready to shoot, not knowing if the basket were five feet away or fifty. The point suddenly becomes very clear. If you don't know where you are going, you cannot bring your talents and abilities into play. Or, to put it differently, to bring your talents into play, you have to know where you are going.

Setting a goal enables you to focus your abilities, to apply them intelligently and effectively, to maximize them to the utmost. As you get closer to a goal, you continue to fine-tune your abilities, and you gather other important abilities and information that you otherwise would be inattentive to.

Often the analogy used is a ship at sea. With a compass, a captain, a crew, and other navigational instruments, a ship can reach a distant harbor over and over again. Yet that same ship, without a destination, without a plan for sailing, and without any devices for measuring progress, would almost certainly be thrashed against rocks and would sink. It would have almost no chance at all of ever arriving safely at some distant port.

Obviously, goals and mapped-out plans are important—for people as well as for ships. Olympic champions, movie stars, business tycoons—nearly all of them set goals and carefully planned their rise to the top of their field.

So, set goals. Map out your plans. Give yourself a step-by-step procedure for attaining your goals, and then go for it! You *can* do it.

Quitting's Not So Bad!

Yes. You can do it. But you can quit before you attain your goals, too. Self-help books usually don't mention this. More likely they say, "Set your goal and don't ever stop until you reach it. A winner never quits, and a quitter never wins."

These are nice phrases, and they can be inspiring. However, another line that is, at times, equally valid is: "Quit while you're ahead."

Did you ever wonder why you can't seem to stick to all the plans and goals you have set for yourself? Why you seem to fade out? Why your effort lags? Why you often give up?

Perhaps you have spent time berating yourself for failures you should be proud of. Yes, proud of. After all, imagine what life would be like if everyone managed to carry out each hair-brained scheme ever devised or decided upon! "Hey, let's call Old Man Johnson every night after midnight!"

I remember vowing as a little boy never to speak to my Dad

again because he yelled at me for something that today I cannot even recall.

How many little kids have decided to become doctors, lawyers, or Indian chiefs? Think of all the cowboys and ballerinas we would have roaming around our streets if all the little would-be rope-masters and toe-dancers had kept to their early desires. The point is, people often don't make good decisions. Yesterday's stupid vow, fortunately, can be changed today. Today's willpower might be overruled by tomorrow's whim—which, often, is as it should be.

In my life, I have heard hundreds of little kids promise to practice basketball until they become NBA stars. But they were destined to be 5 feet 9 inches tall and slow, with no jumping ability. Isn't it wonderful that they lost their commitment to basketball and began putting their time into other things?

It is even wonderful that students abandon commitments to study six hours a night. Studying sounds like a noble idea that should be encouraged. But six hours a night? What if something big is happening? What if a special concert comes to town? Or a special person? Or what if the student takes up a sport? Or makes a new friend? Should the rest of life be decided because one inspired student—or little kid or athlete or adult—once decided to do something?

Why should a decision made at age ten control your life at age sixteen? This is a valid question that points out the need for foresight, for planning, and for not being afraid to change your plans as you go.

"Stick-to-it-iveness," persistence, and dedication are sometimes admirable qualities. Other times, they can be foolish, excessive, or fanatical.

Even though quitting is often berated, it is often the intelligent thing to do. In fact, whenever you find you can use your time more effectively, you should quit what you are doing and do the new thing.

How do you know when it is wise to give up a goal, change a plan, or quit some project? There are no formulas set in stone, but a good guideline would be: Don't decide under duress. Decide in a private space, an "air-conditioned room," giving yourself time to reflect on your options, to weigh the pros and cons.

If you have committed yourself to running a marathon, that may or may not be good for you. You can count on "voices from within" telling you to quit when you are running under a hot summer sun in the midst of your training. Quitting at that time most often would be a concession to laziness, not to intelligent course-adjusting. Of course, there are always exceptions. There may be times when your body or your heart will tell you it is time to stop. But most often, you will not be in a life-threatening situation. You will simply be battling your own natural laziness. That's why you should make your decisions in a quiet, comfortable room, off by yourself, with time to think about the goal you have and the plan you have put together. You believed in it once. Are there good, compelling reasons for thinking differently now? Are you caving in to laziness? Or do you have something more important to do, something that would give you more satisfaction, something you will be proud of later?

This kind of thinking has dozens, hundreds of applications, not just to setting and adjusting your goals, but to your entire life. It is important enough to name it and elaborate . . .

Your Air-Conditioned-Room Response

Learning to live well, to be proud of yourself, of what you do and how you act, requires little more than acting on your commitment to making an air-conditioned-room response to any situation you may encounter.

This response is exactly what it appears to be. It is your carefully thought-out, carefully considered, unpressured, best thinking under ideal conditions. What would you do if you suddenly got a call and were told that you won a lottery? What would you do if you were walking down the street minding your own business and a little kid spit on you? What would you do if a policeman came to your house with handcuffs, to arrest you for a crime you didn't commit? What would you do if you were stranded ten miles from home, out in the country, late at night, in a snowstorm, because your friend's car ran out of gas?

There are not necessarily right and wrong answers to these questions. But thoughtful decisions are possible, carefully weighed and reflectively considered. So are hasty, spur-of-the-moment decisions made with hardly any thought at all. Obviously, the conclusions and courses of action decided upon are likely to be very different from the one method to the other.

So, which method do you want to use? Do you want to go through your life making hasty decisions and constantly looking back, saying, "If only I had had time to think," or "If I had it to do over . . ."

The world is filled with people who wish they could do things over, who wish they had made decisions that took a "longer view," in which the long-term consequences were carefully considered.

You do not need to live your life among those spur-of-the-moment thinkers and "regretters." If you keep in mind the concept of the air-conditioned-room response, it will help you to weigh your options from a better vantage point, even when you don't have much time.

Essentially, the air-conditioned-room response requires you to ask yourself, when confronted with any decision, "Which choice will I be proud of two weeks from now?" You can spend all of your lottery money the first day, you can knock the little kid's teeth out so he will have trouble ever spitting again, you can knock the cop over the head with a lamp—as long as those are the responses you will be truly happy with later.

However, if you have time to sit and think and consider carefully, you may make other decisions. For instance, you may decide to grab the little kid and, instead of spending a lot of time and money in court having to defend your excessively violent attack, you may get him to save you time by making him mow your lawn, rake your leaves, wash your car, or clean your house. Two weeks later, you may be happier to have a clean house, car, or yard than to have attorneys' fees, meetings, court dates, and the satisfaction—is it?—of knowing some little wise-ass spitter is toothless. That's up to you. It is not important that you make the choice that anyone else would. But it is absolutely crucial to your life that you choose something you will be happy with later.

A lot of people have died prematurely because they made hasty decisions to retaliate for some perceived injustice when they had little chance of coming out on top. Better if they had waited, planned their retaliation, carried it out secretly, and lived to enjoy it. Perhaps it would even have been better for them to leave the retaliation to the police and get on with their lives. Maybe, maybe not. No one can tell you how to behave or what to do. But you have to make sure you make decisions that benefit you over the long term, and not just for the moment.

The Ability to Anticipate

Once you understand the importance of meeting each situation with your air-conditioned-room response, you will learn to anticipate the things that are likely to happen to you, and you will prepare in advance a response you will be proud of. How do you want to respond when your teachers, coaches, or parents yell at you for something that is not your fault? You can rant and rave. After all, *they* are wrong, not you. Or, you can relax and explain your innocence clearly and quietly. You can even say nothing at all, accepting the unjust criticism with a sense of smug satisfaction, knowing they're wrong and choosing not to reveal your knowledge until a later time (or never!). It's up to you. Do you want your life suddenly interrupted with a shouting match, just because someone made an error that can be corrected?

If you have prepared a response that you know you will be happy with later, it becomes easier to deliver that response when you have to. Additionally, you will find that many events or happenings you encounter tend to be alike, so you can easily fit an old response to the new situation.

No Preparation, No Response

What if you have failed to anticipate an event and have no response prepared? That's a crucial question, and one you should be prepared for. If you have been too stupid to anticipate an event, you should assume you will be too stupid to respond intelligently. Therefore, you ought to prepare yourself to use what is probably the best response to all unanticipated events: Be quiet, retreat, try to take as little action as possible, and buy yourself some time to think.

Remember, get in the habit of putting the blame on yourself. Too stupid to anticipate? Then too stupid to respond well. Take time to think.

Two Yous: You-the-Thinker and You-the-Robot

With the air-conditioned-room-response philosophy, you are equipped to live the best possible life for you; and you will likely find yourself being able in a short time to anticipate nearly every situation that will happen to you. At the same time, you will likely see yourself in terms of two basic categories: you the anticipator, thinker, planner; and you the actor, doer, robot.

Once you decide something using your best thinking, you have to carry out what you have decided. *Don't second guess yourself under duress.* Learn to separate the doer from the thinker, the robot from the planner. If you have decided unhurriedly in an air-conditioned room to run a mile, then go out and run that mile. Don't think about it while doing it. Trust you-the-thinker to have anticipated the heat, the fatigue, and all the other negative factors, and still have determined that you could do what you decided upon.

Can you do the things you decide upon? Can you think well enough to be able to give yourself doable things to do?

It doesn't make any sense to go through life always making plans and schedules and diets and regimens that you continually fail to carry out. Clearly, if this happens to you, you need to have more awareness of your dual selves, and you need to get them both in line. You-the-thinker has to quit demanding more than can be given; you-the-robot has to start doing the things demanded.

Once it is viewed in this way, life becomes an interesting game. What can you-the-thinker devise that stretches your abilities and enables you to use and develop your talents, yet is doable? And how good are the you-the-robot at suspending the thinking process and merely doing when that time has come?

There are people who make great plans they can never follow, and just as many people who sabotage their own development by failing to carry out plans that could lead them to success.

Who is at fault in your life, the planner or the doer? You really can't lay blame on one or the other. The planner has to be intelligent enough not to give the lazy doer things he or she will fail to do. And the doer has to quit thinking and just do the things he or she is given to do.

It begins to sound like so much double talk because it is! You are a double—two distinct beings who have to learn to live together harmoniously. It is stupid to go through your life making unrealistic demands on yourself, and it is stupid to go through your life berating yourself for laziness.

If you have failed to stick to your last twelve diets, it may be because all were poorly planned. Make the next one easier so success will be possible. Set smaller goals over a shorter period of time. Then you can say, "I stuck to that three-week diet—but did not renew it." Psychically, that is a lot different from having failed to stay on it forever. If you aren't going to be able to do a diet forever, don't demand forever from yourself.

Challenge yourself to think and plan with more and more intelligence, learning to consider *all* the factors that will come into play as you-the-robot tries to carry out the plans. And challenge yourself to carry out those plans and, if they are too difficult, have the robot report back, so the plans get changed. Just don't let the robot do the thinking. The robot has to *do* better; the thinker has to *plan* better.

Getting the thinker and the robot in sync really does become an exciting game, a game from which you can learn and with which you can improve. So, work at this "marriage." It will pay you big dividends.

*Ask people who look concerned
what their plans or aspirations are.
"What are you hoping for these days?"
Or "Do you have any good plans in the works right now?"
Questions like these force people to think about
what you want to hear:
interesting stuff, not a bagful of problems.*

"What's Right?"

One of the most important skills you can develop is the ability to interpret ambiguous things in a positive light.

Down through the years, television—in need of quick action and fast-moving plots—has particularly led people to believe that one small action should lead to suspicion. For example, a guy comes home with lipstick on his collar, and right away his wife or girlfriend flies into a rage. She *knows* he is having an affair, she yells, then slams a door, and runs out to a friend's house or some other lover to "show him."

It may work for television, but such behavior is stupid in real life. What if the guy had embraced an old woman at work because she received a sudden call about the death of a loved one? How stupid the wife's reaction is in that case! Yet people do this kind of thing all the time. And it is hardly limited to suspicious wives. Guys are constantly flying into a rage merely because they call and their wife or girlfriend is not home. Or a guy sees his wife getting out of the car of someone he does not know.

Don't Jump to Conclusions

Jumping to conclusions based on limited information not only is stupid, but is very unattractive. The woman who is outraged over a trace of lipstick is not merely wrong to do that, she is likely to lose completely any respect her man had left for her.

Assume the Best

Whether you are right or wrong is not important in the early stages of any suspicion. Just assume the best. Forget the suspicion. Put it out of your mind. Assume that everything is fine. Later you may find that your suspicions were justified. So what? What do you lose by being patient and taking the time to find out for sure?

Think about your health. You may see one tiny symptom and suddenly assume you have cancer. Then you spend the next ten years worrying about it—and literally destroy yourself with tension and stress. Better to assume you are fine, and let the force of a positive outlook help your body to stay healthy. If there is a real, definite problem, take care of it. Otherwise, forget about it.

A famous poem, *Desiderata,* says it well: Do not distress your-self with imaginings. Make sure only real, concrete things bother you, not mere suspicions of what could or might happen.

Negative Question Equals Negative Response

Think of how important this concept is with regard to communi-cating with others. Suppose you see a friend who looks tense or concerned. The tendency in many people is to ask right away, "What's wrong?"

What kind of answer do they get? They get an answer about all of the things that are wrong. They could just as easily have asked, "What's *right?*" Or, "Do you have any good news?"

Why not give others the opportunity to empty out the good things that are on their minds—or to look for some—instead of asking them to shed their problems and worries? Negative questions elicit negative answers. So why not try to rephrase your questions to bring about positive answers? Ask people who look concerned what their plans or aspirations are. "What are you hoping for these days?" or "Do you have any good plans in the works right now?" Questions like that force people to think about what you want to hear: interesting stuff. Not a bagful of problems.

Interpretation Versus Avoidance

Though it's important to put a positive interpretation on ambiguous events—things that are not yet clear or certain—that does not mean you should walk around chattering positively when all about you is in ruin. For example, if you have flunked five consecutive tests, it is foolish to be telling people you are confident that you will get an A in the class. This is not interpreting ambiguous things positively; it is interpreting *negative* things positively. This is little more than lying to yourself and to others.

If you have one poor performance on a test, this is no reason to push a panic button. Rather, it makes sense to remain optimistic while you find out why you did poorly, taking definite steps to make sure a poor performance is not repeated. If you take these two action steps, you have every reason to be optimistic that you will end up with a good grade.

Be positive. Take action. If you don't have sufficient information to come to a conclusion, don't come to one. Put it off and go on with your life. Instead of looking for cracks in a dam, build a dam of your own.

Many suspicious, nagging people actually drive their friends or mates away, not because other people are so much more attractive, but because negative assumptions, nagging questions, complaints, and suspicions are no fun to listen to constantly. The point is, putting a negative flavor on events is just plain unattractive, besides being unhealthy. If you look for problems that aren't there, you are likely to create some of your own.

Learn instead to see and ask for the best, and many times you will actually be responsible for turning people who are uncertain about their direction toward the positive rather than the negative. Trust and support are not merely wonderful gifts to give another; they can actually influence another's behavior in a positive way. Just like suspicions tend to provoke precisely the actions suspected.

Giving people and events the benefit of the doubt simply makes good sense. It is not a matter of avoiding the facts, but rather an opportunity to shape and influence them.

When something is caught in your throat, your goal is urgently clear.
You want it out so that you can breathe again.
You will try anything—dozens of things—
and being wrong won't bother you one bit.
You will follow each failure with a new, tremendous effort to succeed.

The "Secret" of Success: Piling Up Failures

The secret of success is hardly a secret. It has been clear throughout the centuries, known to generals trying to win wars, to painters trying to produce great art, to scientists trying to discover the ways of nature, to religious leaders trying to convert the unbelievers, to inventors trying to make work or life easier.

The secret, as the title of this chapter indicates, is not to possess some mysterious formula, but rather to be willing to pile up failures in pursuit of a goal.

Imagine for a moment you have something caught in your throat and suddenly are unable to breathe. Would you pick up the Yellow Pages, look up "Throat Blockage," and then try to decide from the advertisements which companies were most effective? Would you sit down with a pen and clipboard and make a long list of possible alternatives? Of course not! When something really matters to you, when your goal is urgently clear, when you not only know what you want but want it badly, you will try one thing and another and another; and you will keep trying until you get what you must have.

When something is caught in your throat, your goal is urgently clear. You want it out so that you can breathe again. You will try anything—dozens of things—and being wrong won't bother you one bit. You will follow each failure with a new, tremendous effort to succeed. If you think it will work, you will stand on your head, beat your own neck, or hurl yourself to the ground. In pursuit of this goal, you will endure the laughter of onlookers, the scorn of friends—anything—to get the blockage out of your throat.

Yeah, okay, you've got the idea. But some of you are saying, "Real goals are different." And you know what? You are wrong. Real goals are not different. At least they wouldn't look that way in the heads of Thomas Edison, Julius Caesar, Pablo Picasso, Jesus Christ, or Galileo Galilei. The great ones—but not just the great ones—pursue their dreams with the same urgency and the same sense of purpose and commitment that you would pursue clearing your throat. Laugh at them, tell them their methods won't work, but they will not be dissuaded. Like someone with a blocked throat, they try their best over and over again, until they get what they want—or die trying.

Burning Desire

Do you need to ask why you have difficulty succeeding? Can you imagine what competition really means? Imagine you are in a race against someone who wants victory the way you want that obstruction out of your throat. That would be one furious competitor!

So what is the secret of success? More than anything, it is desire. How much desire must you have to succeed? When the day comes that you suddenly have an absolutely burning desire to do something, you will do it. Forget this book, forget the clipboard, forget the Yellow Pages. You will try and try and do and do, until you get there, learning from each mistake because the feeling inside is urgent. Nothing else really matters.

What if few of your goals are life-and-death kinds of things? Welcome to the club, welcome to the world. You are like most everyone else. You might not have the lofty goals of a Galileo, a Caesar, or a Christ—people willing to die for their goals—but this does not relegate you to total failure.

What you need to do is learn from the great examples, and adopt as many of their principles as you can.

The most important of these is the willingness to try and fail, try and fail, try and fail. And to make each successive attempt as enthusiastic, as hopeful, as full of effort as the first.

Not a Matter of Life and Death

Typically, those of us with less than a life-and-death commitment to our undertakings try something a couple of times and, if we don't succeed, let our effort and enthusiasm droop. We may try a few more times, but our engines are no longer running at full tilt. We are no longer all eyes and ears, we don't have our very pores open, struggling to absorb information so that the next try will be successful. That is what you must make a conscious effort to change. And you can do it with knowledge and pride.

Let's face it. We can't approach every goal with a life-and-death attitude. And that's probably a good thing, isn't it? All sorts of people would be dying for marble games, for jacks, for yoyos and tops. Every whim imaginable would become someone's life-and-death goal. People would be jumping off buildings, hurling themselves in front of trains by the millions!

So, no, you do not have to berate yourself for having no burning, life-and-death desires at this moment. Live a little, do some things. The right goal will present itself. Be patient. And in the meantime, while you wait, fill your life with some activity, some achievements, even if they happen not to be heroic.

Fine. So you choose a goal instead of having it choose you. And you decide to pursue it with dedication. Use your knowledge of how great people attack their goals to see how closely you can parallel their efforts. Even though you are not willing to die for your goal, you want to mimic their success principles as much as possible— and you can.

You can learn to pile up failures gratuitously, in other words, by expecting them, welcoming them, knowing they will come, and therefore not letting them have a negative influence on your next efforts. Try, fail, learn from your mistakes. How willing are you to pile up failures gratuitously, benignly, without concern for them, without anguish, with an open-arms, almost friendly kind of acceptance?

If you are willing to work hard at something and willing to fail often along the way without experiencing a drop in your level of enthusiasm, then you will succeed at most of the things you attempt.

Do you want a date with a great looking person? Ask one. Ask another. Ask another. Figure on eight being "the charm." You've heard the saying, "three's a charm," but figure on eight. Give yourself some leeway. Keep trying—and make sure each effort, each request, is as enthusiastic as the first.

Do you want to be a successful salesperson? Introduce yourself, become the prospect's friend, make your pitch, show your goods, and ask for the money. Didn't work? Find another prospect. Introduce yourself, become the prospect's friend, make your pitch, show your goods, and ask for the money. Didn't work? Find another, and another. Improve your presentation. Ask every person who turned down your pitch what you could have done better, and learn from them—then try again. And again, and again.

Is the secret of success becoming abundantly clear to you? Thomas Edison learned five hundred ways *not* to make a light bulb before he found the right one. Abraham Lincoln, one of our greatest presidents, lost seven or eight minor elections on his way to the presidency. (No one thought he was "on his way" but Lincoln himself.) Nearly every author—famous and unknown—has received dozens of rejections before finding someone who would publish his or her first book.

How to Become a Millionaire

How many examples do you need? Even winning a lottery requires that willingness to try and try again—to plunk down that forty-sixth dollar with the same hope and enthusiasm you had when you plunked down the first. Have you ever read about big lottery winners? Multimillionaires? Have you ever noticed how few of them say, "That was the first contest I ever entered"? Nearly all of them say that they have entered often, for years, every day. In other words, even to win a totally "lucky" thing like a lottery takes persistence, dedication, the willingness to pile up failures gratuitously, and to make each new effort the best one possible. Think some more about this crazy example of the lottery winners. It's totally luck, supposedly, but the winners rarely claim they just chose some numbers out of a hat. Nearly all of them have a system they believe in. They have lucky numbers; perhaps their sons' birth dates or their wedding anniversary, or the closing figure of the Dow Jones Industrials. They don't just stick any old numbers on the page as they plunk down their dollars. They play numbers with a special meaning, numbers they love, numbers that give them a hunch or a good feeling. And they play them with enthusiasm, time and time again.

What a lesson! Even in the crazy, one-in-a-billion business of lottery playing, the big winners constantly apply the principles of the greats. Learn to fail often, and imbue each successive attempt with enthusiasm and effort.

Not a Tale of a Fiery Crash

It would be possible to end this chapter with dozens of stories of Olympic champions or historical figures who overcame great odds to go on to victory. Instead I'll tell you the story of a pilot living in Utah. It is not going to be the tale of some near-fatal air crash or of saving the day in the nick of time. It's an undramatic vacation tale with no punch line. But it is inspiring nevertheless.

The guy has made a commitment to fill his life with action. Two of his most recent commitments were to learn to speak Spanish and to learn to play golf. So he combined the two and took a weekend trip to Mexico. He studied Spanish in a school there and went off golfing one afternoon, with his fine new golf clubs, leather bag, new balls, new tees, golf hat, golf glove, the whole bit, you might say.

The course was virtually empty except for dozens of laborers sitting around. Everyone was watching this American who had come to golf. He had a caddy assigned to him, and the workers were moved off the tee and greens that they had been cutting by hand. (There were no lawn mowers; machinery was scarce but labor was cheap and abundant.) So dozens watched as he swung at the first ball, missed, and sent a clump of dirt and grass flying twenty yards down the fairway. The Mexicans rolled their eyes and looked at each other with amusement. But they didn't laugh out loud. The caddy was hoping for a big tip, and they all knew that laughing at a client was not the way to make that happen. But they restrained their laughter with difficulty as the pilot swung and missed again, as another clump of grass went sailing toward the horizon.

There is no punch line. The guy had every right to be embarrassed. He had all that expensive equipment and he couldn't golf worth a hoot. All those people were watching him and all he was doing was tearing up their beautiful course. His third grand swing topped the ball and sent it rolling a few feet off the tee, at which time he handed his caddy his driver and asked—in his best Spanish—for an "Uno iron!" He played all eighteen holes, no doubt gathering something of a crowd hidden among the trees as he walked from hole to hole, hitting as much grass as ball.

It is a scenario few people would be willing to endure for fun, on vacation, because of a commitment to do things, to fill life with actions and attempts and new things. It is funny, perhaps foolish, and certainly not a matter of life and death. But it is inspiring nevertheless. It is an everyday example of the stuff success is made of.

Had we begun this chapter with the notion that a person could be standing in water and rats, in a deep dark pit, with no possible help to get out, yet feel a sense of excitement, you probably would have said it was impossible.

Pit Mentality

Imagine for a moment falling into a pit—a deep, dark, damp, rat-infested pit. There is no one to help you get out, no rope to cling to, nothing. You are down there, it is night, and you know that no help is on the way. It's terrible, no ifs, ands, or buts. It's so terrible, in fact, that your mind quickly assimilates the experience. Even the rats. Just one rat running through your living room would be cause for alarm. But here there are dozens scurrying at your feet. There really isn't a possibility of alarm. It's suddenly a condition of life. The revulsion won't last long. You can't even kill yourself at the bottom of a deep dark pit. Giving up wouldn't occur to even the most cowardly of us—because that would mean having rats run over your face, instead of just over your shoes.

Do you know what nearly every human in the world would do in this circumstance—cowardly and courageous alike? In nice sociological terms, they would gain control of the environment. They would stomp their feet and make it clear to the rats to stay away.

You might run out of your house if just one rat entered your living room, but if a dozen scurried at your feet in the pit, you would assert yourself. You would make it clear who was the most powerful. And soon, most of the rats would stay clear of you.

Next, you would look for a way out. You would feel the walls.

And you would search the floors for an instrument—a light, a stick, or a rope—something that might help you get out of there.

Finding nothing, you would once again feel the walls. You would push at them, scratch at them, dig at them, pausing here and there to reassert your dominion over the rats at your feet.

You would be active. Your mind would search for a way out. You would dig your hands into the walls of the pit. When some earth came away in your hands, you would feel a sudden sense of excitement. It just might be possible to dig notches all the way up the wall and climb out.

Think about that. Had we begun this chapter with the notion that a person could be standing in water and rats, in a dark pit, with no possible help to get out, yet feel a sense of excitement, you probably would have said it was impossible. Yet you would feel it yourself in this situation, just like everyone else.

What made the difference? The hope of getting out; the belief that it could be done; a plan in mind; and a first step already taken.

In the very worst of circumstances, one notch and a plan are all that anyone needs to feel excitement. This ought to speak to you loudly and clearly about the importance of having a goal and a plan and a way to move toward a better situation, a better life.

"Setting goals" and "making plans" are not merely nice sociological terms confined to books on self-help and motivation. They are the keys to peace of mind and contentedness. You may think you don't need them—and at times you may not. But for the most part, they are the keys to happiness in life.

You can change your goals and plans constantly. But you ought to have some with you always.

When you sink into the doldrums, you can almost be sure that the cause is a lack of vision, an inability to see where your efforts are leading you.

You can be on the top of a mountain, sitting in a Turkish bath, with diamonds around you, servants, and food fit for a king. You can *be* a king—and still be less excited than the person knee-deep in water and rats.

The difference is a sense of purpose, a plan of action, a knowledge of where you are going, particularly an awareness that you are on an upward path. Hard work with a purpose is satisfying, even energizing—whereas even easy work without a purpose is enervating.

The king at the top of the mountain is hardly going to feel terrific if his power is on the decline, if he is slipping downward. In other words, what matters is not where you *are* but in what direction you are *heading.*

If you are depressed, chances are you have lost sight of where you are headed or how you can get out. It may be time to revise your plans or make new ones. Spend your time feeling the walls, seeking a way. Because once you have discovered a way out—no matter how hard it is, no matter what your circumstances are—you will be energized again.

Even at rock bottom, at the bottom of a pit, sunk to your lowest level, there is a way out. Forget about where you were, what should have been or could have been or might have been, and look ahead to where you want to be. No doubt there is a way to get there, or at least a way to get to some better place.

Then start digging. The work, surprisingly, is the easiest part— once you know where you are going and have a plan that will get you there.

*Failure isn't a consideration when you aren't even trying.
Had Tom jumped forty-seven times, there is no question that he
would have gotten many balls. Other kids, who couldn't leap well
at all, just happened to be where the balls came down.*

7-47: Injecting Your Abilities into the Fray, or Being Where the Balls Come Down

7-47. Sounds like a big airplane, but it is a statistic. A tough kid, a high school athlete with an exceptional ability to jump, was at an all-star basketball camp hoping to show off his skills to college coaches so he could get a scholarship.

As director of the camp, I had the opportunity to watch the kid play and then comment on his performance in a general session the next day. The comments may seem initially surprising.

"Tom, I watched you carefully yesterday. In fact, I kept a statistic sheet on you during the first half of the game. You knew college coaches were in the stands, didn't you?"

Tom nodded.

"And you wanted to impress them, didn't you?"

Again, a nod.

"And you're proud of your leaping ability, aren't you? You don't have to be embarrassed to admit it. You have a 34-inch vertical leap. That's better than any of the 280 kids here. You can jump, and college coaches are here to see jumpers. They want guys who can jump. You know that, don't you?"

Tom nodded again. The rest of the group waited for the point.

"In the first half yesterday, I counted forty-seven times when there was an opportunity to leap, an opportunity to go up for a rebound and show everyone in the gym who was the highest jumper in camp. You know how many times you leaped in the first half, Tom?"

He didn't know. The question seemed to take him by surprise.

"*Seven.* Seven times out of forty-seven. That's about one-seventh of the time. How do you expect to impress anyone while showing off your skills one-seventh of the time?"

Although I brought this up to impress upon Tom the importance of using his ability, I could have pointed to anyone in the room and cited a similar statistic. All the boys at the camp were there to show off their abilities, but few of them had sufficient awareness of their opportunities to do so. Had someone prevented Tom from leaping forty times, he might have been outraged. But left on his own, he lost forty chances himself.

The point was particularly important to me, so I went on.

"Tom, I don't mean to make fun of you. What I have just said really applies to everyone here, except that not everyone here has as good an opportunity to show off as you do. Many of us could perhaps get in position to leap forty-seven times, yet we would get only a few balls, because we just don't jump high enough to get very many. You, on the other hand, would get just about every one you leaped for. In other words, you could become more accomplished than the rest of us, so you are in that sense the most guilty.

"However, what if this were a writing camp instead of a basketball camp? The director of the writing camp could be up here, and I would be one of the students out where you are, and the guy would wag his finger in my face and say, 'DeVenzio, what's wrong with you? Didn't you win a big essay contest in high school? Didn't you impress all your professors in college with your writing ability? Why haven't you written a couple of successful books by now? *What are you doing with your ability now?*' "

" 'You have some talent, and you don't bother using it. How can you be so foolish? What good is a talent if you don't use it?' I am as guilty as you, Tom. If I embarrassed you with my 7-47 statistic, I have now embarrassed myself. You don't have a good reason for not jumping more often. I don't have a good reason for not writing every day. I think it's time that both of us made a commitment. You better start leaping out there on the court, and I'm going to start writing more."

It was more than a talk, it was a commitment in front of 280 high-school basketball players. "Come back next summer," I told them, "and I will have finished a book, maybe two."

This book is my promise to them, and it is the product of that 7-47 talk—the realization that if you can jump, you should jump. If you can write, you should write. You don't have to be the best leaper in the camp. Certainly I am not the best of writers. But you are not going to get anywhere keeping the talents you do have in your pocket. You have to get them "out there." You have to inject them into the fray, into the world, into life.

The actual definition of "fray" is a "noisy quarrel," probably a good way to think about life—and a lot like those basketball games in which Tom was failing to inject himself sufficiently. Neither those games nor life wait around for you to inject yourself. The pace is fast; the opportunities present themselves and then disappear. And there is so much noise, so many distractions, that you can go through the whole thing—the game, or life itself—without anyone really noticing how many missed opportunities are occurring. Tom had no idea he was showing off at a 7-for-47 clip—just as it had not occurred to me, until making a point to Tom, that whatever ability I have as a writer was going completely to waste. I hadn't even given any publishers the chance to turn me down, since I hadn't submitted anything.

The guilty are everywhere. Singers don't sing. Piano players don't play. Athletes don't try out for teams. Readers don't open books.

If you pause long enough to make a list of your talents, and to note the opportunities when and where they may be used, you will likely be as appalled at your failures as Tom and I were at ours.

You cannot inject yourself into a noisy quarrel by sitting quietly in the back of the room. Isn't it time you moved to the front and raised your voice, made your opinion heard, and injected your abilities into the fray?

Failure isn't a consideration when you aren't even trying. Had Tom jumped forty-seven times, there is no question he would have gotten many balls. Many of them were grabbed by smaller kids who couldn't leap well at all; they just happened to be where the balls came down.

You could be getting some of that action.

*The road to success is not a straight line traveled by
great thinkers who are careful not to make any mistakes.
Instead it is a jagged maze of wrong paths taken by persistent doers.*

Do Things

The advice of this chapter repeats that of other chapters. Sometimes, it is necessary to repeat things or say them in a variety of ways, to make sure they sink in.

The point of this chapter is *the* secret of success itself. How to achieve success is the subject of book after book, tape after tape, speech after speech. But none of them can give a whole lot more advice than the following:

Do things.

Success at anything is a lot more like learning to ride a bike than anyone usually wants to admit. People can give you every sort of technical advice, but the facts are that no one ever stays on a bike on the first try, regardless of who is teaching or of how talented the beginner is.

Throw in diagrams, graph paper, computer printouts, and a team of scientists, and little kids still have to get on bikes and fall to one side, then the other. Their bodies and minds simply have to make some mistakes—and learn from them—and keep working together until finally riding is effortless. Forget all the talk, forget all the technique. Do.

Therefore, this chapter is going to be very short, to make sure we do not obscure the point. Do you want to be successful? Do things.

Do things.

Let me close this with one simple definition of stupid and smart people seeking success.

Stupid people sit around trying to think up the best possible way to do something, and rarely ever try at all.

When smart people do something and mess up, they do it again. If they mess up again, they do it again, each time learning from their past mistakes. They do and do and do and do and do, over and over and over, making mistake after mistake, until they finally have it right.

The road to success is not a straight line traveled by thinkers careful not to make a mistake. Instead it is a jagged maze of wrong paths taken by persistent doers.

Once you understand this concept fully, you will be free to act upon your ideas—and you will be able to understand easily the inherent contradiction of a thirty-six-line poet.

Confused? Read on. . . .

Visiting her bedroom was as distant a possibility as her writing
"The Rime of the Ancient Mariner." She had no plans
to write a thousand poems, and we suddenly had no plans
to get together again.

What's a Poet?

"I made the mistake of being honest—eventually. Actually, I had tried very hard to lie."

She said she was an aspiring poet, and she wanted to know if I would read her poems sometime and tell her what I thought. No doubt she had already received a lot of positive feedback from people when she told them the poet thing. Not too many people are poets these days.

Better yet, if you really want to make people sit up and take notice, call yourself a philosopher. There are virtually none of those.

Anyway, her line worked on me. Why shouldn't it? She was gorgeous. I wanted to get along with her, wanted to flatter her—and so did every other man who saw her. So when she hit me with this poet thing, I acted impressed, and I was.

So anyway, I went to her place to read her poems.

"What do you think?" she asked, after I had pored over them long enough to have read each one five or six times. I knit my brow, mumbled some lines half out loud, and appeared to have explored every nook and cranny and subtlety of each line.

"They're good," I said, "they're good. I like them."

I said it with all the force and sincerity I could muster.

"No, really," she said, "what do you *really* think?"

"I like them," I said unhesitatingly. "I really do. They're good. I liked that line about the candle, and the one about the flower rising like a sun."

I tried to throw in some actual examples, so she would know I was serious. "Yeah, they're good, they're good."

I never did know why I couldn't lie better, why my mother could always tell by the look on my face.

Why did this beautiful woman have to press me? I said I liked her stuff, it was good, yeah, real good. Can't we just go into your bedroom now and enjoy life together? I didn't want to act too eager, especially because it was clear she was not at all finished discussing poetry.

"What do you really think?" she asked once more. How did *she* know I had other thoughts I had not yet revealed?

Finally, she asked one more time, and I broke.

"Show me some others," I said.

"These are all I have," she answered.

All you have, I thought. How could those be all you have? Didn't you tell me you spent many evenings working on your poetry? What the hell were you doing all that time?

I didn't say any of that. But I was surprised. She had three tiny poems, each about eight to sixteen lines, and she'd been calling herself a poet.

"You must have some others," I said finally.

"No," she said. "I've been working to get these just right, before I go on to any others. Why worry about others? What do you think about these?"

My patience had run out. I forgot my goal of getting into her bedroom, and just became myself. "Look," I said, "what's the use of having three perfect poems?" Actually I was thinking, "Sun glistening on the dew-sparkled blossoms of spring"! These are not going to become perfect poems. That's eighth-grade stuff. I mean, nothing against eighth graders, but everyone who ever sat down to write a poem came up with stuff at least as good as hers. She had a "flickering light fading in the night," a "flower drinking the rain," a "mystical orange dawn." How was anyone going to get excited about that?

"Look," I said, "these are okay. I like them, I don't particularly like them, it doesn't matter. What you need to do is to write a thousand poems. Then I can look through them and hate five hundred of them and be indifferent about two hundred of them and think a hundred aren't bad—and still have two hundred that I kind of like. If you give me time to look at all thousand of them, chances are I'll like fifty of them a lot—and *that's a book of poems.* Do you understand? A poet is someone who has written a thousand poems. That way, everyone in the world is likely to appreciate some of it. You just can't be a poet with three short poems. You can't *expect* anyone to like just three."

"So, you don't like them, do you?" she asked.

"That's not the point, goddammit," I said. "I wouldn't like any given three poems of Robert Frost or Walt Whitman. Does that mean they aren't good poets?"

She thought I was using some sophisticated bullshit to obfuscate (she actually used that word!) my true feelings.

"Obfuscate, my ass," I said. "My true feelings are exactly what I'm saying they are. I don't particularly like your three poems, but that isn't at all important. The best poet in the world could show me three poems that I would think were awful. That's a given, that's life, and that's no big deal. Because, at the same time, there isn't a poet in the world I can't appreciate—if they just show me a thousand poems. I *know* I'll find some I like out of a thousand. I know I'll get some new insights and be delighted by some phrases and some juxtapositions I never thought of before—and I'll truly appreciate that. It won't bother me one bit that I disliked a hundred poems, if I take away some memorable lines and some new insights."

She had this frown on her face. She felt personally belittled or attacked. She was no longer attractive to me, she thought. And she was definitely no longer attracted to me. The glow had gone from her face. Visiting her bedroom was as distant a possibility as her writing "The Rime of the Ancient Mariner." She had no plans to write a thousand poems, and we suddenly had no plans to get together again. A potentially wonderful relationship with a truly gorgeous creature was smashed on the rocks of a golden dawn while dew-sparkled blossoms littered the wreckage of my hopes.

Perhaps I should have asked a hundred questions, turned her phrases over and over and joined her fully—a poet of the senses and of the swirling mind and of the cocktail-party circuit. Why did

I have to go and let truth and personal beliefs get in the way of extracurricular activities?

But alas, I think you got the point. A poet doesn't work on three poems, trying for years to perfect them. A poet writes poems. A poet writes a thousand poems. A runner runs a thousand miles.

Until you've filled a thousand pages with verse, or a thousand miles with your footprints, you aren't a poet, or a runner; you're a dreamer.

Had this woman simply told me she'd been working on dreaming, I would have understood perfectly. And we would probably be sleeping together this very moment!

Just don't fool yourself. If you want to be a poet, don't worry or even think about anyone's opinion until you've written a thousand poems. Get to work. Produce.

If you've written a thousand poems, you're a poet. If you've fixed a thousand cars, you're a mechanic—but don't dare go into business after having worked on one car. It just doesn't work that way . . . not even at dawn, when the winds gently blow across the golden plains, and the first signs of spring leap skyward from the meadow.

Okay, so I'm not a poet, either.

*They don't realize that reading is not merely something
done for enjoyment, in a hammock, as a hobby on a Sunday afternoon.
It is a way to learn about yourself and the world,
and a way to turn ropes and swords and trees into elephants.*

Book 'em, Dan-o!

A few lines of verse, if they can even be called that, contain perhaps the best advice we can take with us through life. Sometimes the lines appear in a religious context, sometimes not. But regardless of the context, the lines make abundant good sense:

> Lord, grant me the courage to change what I can,
> The serenity to accept what I cannot,
> and the wisdom to know the difference.

Is there an injustice that outrages you? Can you do something about it? Do you have the courage to talk to people about it, to try to influence public opinion, to try to mobilize people and overcome the incredible force of inertia?

It takes courage to change what you can, to persist, to strive, to work, and to keep trying when it is so easy to give up.

"It's hard," so many people say. So what? Everything's hard.

Somewhere along the line, to be truly satisfied in your life and to fulfill your potential, you have to overcome some hard things and prevail when it is easier to give up. People run marathons, wake up early and jog before work, do all sorts of things as matters of self-discipline. It is important to be able to bend your body to the will of your mind. Work on it. Develop the power to get things done, to lay out a plan and stick to it, thereby bringing to bear on a problem or task a concerted effort over a period of time.

A concerted effort over a period of time—*that* is the courage to make something happen, to change what you can.

On the other hand is the serenity to accept what you cannot change. No amount of work or effort will keep you or your loved ones from dying. Understanding the fact of human mortality is the ultimate form of acceptance. You cannot live forever. Neither can you kiss every woman, or make love to every man; you cannot have everything, no matter how rich you are. Acceptance is part of life. You can become skilled at some things, not at others. You can win some things, but you will lose others.

It cannot be a shock that some things will go wrong in your life, that you will sometimes be sick, that your plans will go awry. That is serenity, acceptance. It is a significant advance over the immature person who constantly asks, "Why me?" But even if you make that advance, even if you learn to accept "the slings and arrows of outrageous fortune," you aren't "there" yet.

The clincher, the line that gives those words real power, what you *really* need is the wisdom to know the difference—the difference between courage and serenity. How do you know when to battle on, forge ahead, keep trying, "never give up"? And how do you know when to stop? How do you know when you are butting your head against a brick wall and have no chance for success?

There are no easy answers. Wisdom does not come easily. It comes from trying, persisting, losing, winning, learning over the long run what you can do, what you cannot do, what is possible and what is impossible. And possibilities constantly change. What you cannot do today, perhaps you can do tomorrow. But then again, you may never again be able to do what you could do yesterday. Professional athletes, for example, are all faced with this dilemma as they get older. How do they accept that their skills are eroding? Are their skills truly eroding, or are they merely victimized by a traditional way of thinking that says they are getting older, therefore their skills must decline? People called "great" throughout history are those who have shown others that things that were thought impossible were actually possible—like running a mile in less than four minutes. However, history is also filled with people labeled "crazy" for trying to prove the impossible, for example, that a net could be strung across the ocean (to keep planes from crashing), or that a man could keep himself in the air by flapping his arms. Flying? That's ridiculous. Then again, who were the Wright brothers? Who fashioned the first successful parachute? How many earlier parachutes had failed?

What is admirable persistence leading to great deeds? And what is foolhardy ignorance leading to wasted or negative effort—or death?

Within that question is the reason we read and think, and study a variety of subjects, even those that initially seem useless. Only by learning a great deal can you make intelligent decisions based on broad-based information.

The story of the six blind men touching an elephant is instructive in this regard. One felt the tail and called it a rope; one felt the side and called it a wall; one felt a leg and called it a tree trunk; one felt an ear and called it a fan; one felt a tusk and called it a sword; and one felt the trunk and called it a snake.

By seeing or knowing just a tiny part of the whole, you are doomed to draw wrong conclusions.

Suddenly the value of reading becomes obvious. How many adults or kids have you heard say, "I don't like reading"? They haven't even read enough to know they are condemning themselves to a narrow life. They don't realize that reading is not merely something done for enjoyment, in a hammock, as a hobby on a Sunday afternoon. It is a way to learn about yourself and the world, and a way to turn ropes and swords and trees into elephants.

Courage, serenity, wisdom. And elephants? You don't expect these things to lead to reading. But they do.

How else are you going to go through life with any hope of knowing the difference between a rope and an elephant's tail? For tens of thousands of kids sitting in the backs of classrooms talking jive, or throwing paper airplanes, or, worse yet, not in school at all, there is little chance that they will make good choices and decisions for their lives. They might understand the lesson of the blind men and the elephant, yet never guess that they are even more deprived.

2

Study Smarter, Not Harder: How to Be Successful in School

There are seven-year-olds who can sing dozens of songs.
Are they geniuses? Hardly. Usually, they have a record or cassette.
They hear the song a few times and soon
it is embedded in their memories.
They know it without trying.

How to Remember What You Study

Before we get into how to remember what you study, let's look at how *not* to do it. Cramming is what most students do. They put off studying till the last possible moment, then go crazy, drink coffee or take pills to stay awake, and try to force all sorts of facts and information into their brains on the night before the exam.

If you have no choice, that is one thing. But most students do have a choice. Planning, self-discipline, and scheduling are precisely the things that are going to make you successful in life. Why not realize that school is preparation for life? Why not realize that putting everything off till the last minute and cramming under pressure at the end is not the way to live, nor is it any way to get the most out of college or books or your courses?

If you prefer that method, you probably ought to get a job and put off getting an education until you learn the value it can have for you. Learning can be enjoyable, but you have to give it a chance to be. Taking pills and cramming after putting off studying is not much different from starving yourself for three days and then eating like a pig on the fourth day. It makes sense to work toward achieving a balance in your eating habits and in your work habits.

The Snatch-and-Reinforce Method of Studying

Without question, the best way to recall what you study is by periodic reinforcement, by snatching short periods of time to study. Five minutes here, ten minutes there, a half hour there. Short periods of time are typically energizing. You don't have time to be bored. There isn't time for your mind to wander. There isn't time for the material to become routine, to "go in one ear and out the other."

Snatch short periods throughout each day, and the material will stick. Consider your knowledge of any popular song you hear on the radio. No one really ever had to, or has to, teach you a song. You hear it a few times, you remember it. There are seven-year-olds who can sing dozens of songs. Are they geniuses? Hardly. Usually, they have a record or cassette. They hear the song a few times and soon it is embedded in their memories. They know it without trying.

The same goes for recalling facts and information from a book. If you just stash it once in your short-term memory, there is always a danger it will escape you. But the material that gets reinforced goes into long-term storage. It stays longer, is tied to a number of other memories, and can be recalled easily.

Put some material on notecards every morning, look through those notecards several times throughout the day, and you will be surprised at how much you can recall without really ever having studied.

The Two-Nights-Before Method

Another process of which you should be aware is reminiscence, the act of recalling events or information. Studies have proved that you can recall information studied two nights before a test better than you can recall the same information studied the night before. I believe this claim, because I have tested it. I had heard about this while in college, and I tried out both methods—studying the night before a test, and studying two nights before. Although one person cannot know with certainty, I felt confident enough in the two-nights-before method that I used it throughout my junior and senior years, and I am convinced that studying two nights before is far superior. Of course, for your own peace of mind, you can always study two nights before and then browse over your main notes the night before, which adds the snatch-and-reinforce method on top of the two-nights-before method.

You may wonder how studying two nights before could possibly be better than studying the night before. It might seem as though you forget things gradually over time; therefore, the longer it has been since you studied something, the easier it is to forget it. The fallacy in this way of thinking is that it fails to take into account reminiscence, which is a basic function of the memory.

"Contents of Package May Have Settled During Shipping"

Most everyone has opened a package from a grocery store and felt sort of cheated because the package is little more than half full. Often, there is an explanation on the side of the package: "This product is sold by weight, not by volume. It has been packed automatically. If the box appears to be less than full, it is because the contents of the package may have settled during shipping."

The contents may have "settled." It appears your mind works similarly. Fill it with dozens—or hundreds—of facts, thousands of words, drawings, associations, and so forth, and it gets filled up. It resists adding more information. It is on "overload." It doesn't want to take any more in, and it hasn't yet had an opportunity to file all the information in the proper places.

Your mind works like a card catalog. It doesn't take a new fact and just stick it in a drawer somewhere. It puts that fact in every drawer, in every file it may pertain to. Thus, "bear" might go under "zoo," under "shit in woods," under "Chicago," under "naked," under "rug by the fireplace," and under many other categories. Like a computer, the mind's processing function works fast, but not instantaneously. Hundreds of pages of information cannot be filed properly in one night. Give the brain an extra night to work on the material and it will be filed by then, and more readily available for recall.

If you have put off everything and have to cram on the last night, go ahead. But know that you have made a conscious decision to do much less than your best. Your best involves studying throughout the term and looking over the material from time to time throughout the semester, so that when you see it again two nights before the final exam, it will not appear new. It will be familiar, easy to assimilate, easy to recall.

Clearly, if you want to succeed the easy way, you will become a better planner, scheduler, and browser. You will snatch a few minutes before each class just to flip through the pages already covered in your textbook, or to flip through pages of the notes you took last week or last month. Using this method, you can *browse* your way to success without ever having to experience that drudgery so often associated with college and with exam-time.

When you sit down on a Thursday evening thinking that you have six or eight hours of studying to do to prepare you for a Friday-morning exam, you must know that you not only have drudgery ahead, but also that you have chosen the worst possible method of preparing yourself.

"We are here to play football, but we have to take some classes,
so here we are, a couple of minutes late
(so we can be in here the shortest possible amount of time)
and sitting as far from you as possible."

Seat Selection

I first recognized the importance of seat selection when I was a student at Duke University. It may seem like a small matter, but I think it is absolutely crucial. I remember walking into class the first day in a course that was considered rather easy, and six or seven members of the football team walked into class a couple of minutes late and headed directly for the last row of seats.

Did they really think they could hide back there? They were inches taller and on the average probably fifty to a hundred pounds heavier than everyone else in the class. And by heading directly to the back, they were telling the professor: "We are here to play football, but we have to take some classes, so here we are, a couple of minutes late (so we can be in here the shortest possible amount of time), and sitting as far from you as possible."

If they thought their seat selection was saying anything else, they were wrong. I took their selection that way, and I wasn't even a professor. I was an athlete just like them, but on the basketball team. Nevertheless, I immediately could feel what the professor was feeling.

They could claim they headed for the back because they didn't want to sit in front of smaller people and block their view, but that excuse doesn't make it. If the professor had been passing out money up front, they would have been more than happy to use their size and strength to get to the front; and they would have come in early, too.

Unless you are *trying* to make a bad impression, you should make it a point to treat each professor's class as though money is being given away. In other words, come early, stay late, and sit as close to the front as possible. If you are extremely tall, sit in the front row on the side. But never choose a back seat unless you wish the professor to assume that you are only there because you have to be.

It isn't very hard to distinguish between students who are eager to be in a class and those who are just there because they have to be. If you are in the latter category, you had better learn to pretend. Remember the money. Come early, stick around late, sit in the front, and watch and listen carefully.

You will be surprised at how much you learn and how much easier it is to pay attention when there is nothing between you and the professor but a few feet of air and no distractions.

Playing "hard ball" in the park
was all that kid was ever going to be doing.
He had lost sight of the intangibles.
He had forgotten (or never understood)
that teams—and personal relationships—
are built on more than practical skill.
Communication and respect, offered in little ways,
play an important part.

Making the Professor Your Friend

Do you already know that an essential ingredient of success in school or in college is making all of your teachers or professors your friends?

Stupid students mumble that some A student is a "brownie" for talking to the teacher. They haven't learned what life—or school—is all about. No doubt there are stupid workers who mumble about fellow workers doing what the boss wants, as though that, too, is stupid. Or athletes mumbling about an athlete on the rise, because he or she tries to impress the coach by coming to practice early, staying late, and doing what the coach asks while in practice.

Stupid? Wise up. People on a success track, people trying to get ahead, people trying to move up some ladder understand that you need the help of those above you. This doesn't mean you have to compromise all your standards or become a brown-nose. It simply means you have to have a healthy respect for what helps people get to where they want to be.

I knew a basketball player who wanted very badly to make his high school team, but during the summer he never went to the "open gym" sessions his coach provided, though his teammates played there three nights a week.

"Why aren't you going?" I asked him.

"Oh, they waste a lot of time there. Those guys talk to the coach and ask him what they need to work on to improve, and it's just a bunch of bullshit. I like to go to the park where the guys are playing hard, man. At the park, guys be goin' crazy, man. Lose a game, you sit for an hour waiting to play again. Guys be playin' for keeps there."

"How are they playing for keeps if they have to sit out for an hour?" I asked.

"You play hard and win, you don't have to sit out."

"So, do you always win?"

"Not always, but most of the time," he said. "When we get to tryouts, man, I'm gonna show those guys and the coach what it means to play *hard* ball."

"Yeah," I said, "and the coach is going to show you what it means to get cut. Or to sit on the pines, the bench. You know, man, like splinters in your butt!"

You get the idea. Who was this kid fooling but himself? If you want to be on the team, you'd better practice where the coaches can see you, you better let them know that you want to play, you'd better talk to them, ask how you can improve, and you'd better ask what they are looking for and how things should be done.

Playing "hard ball" in the park was all that kid was ever going to be doing. He had lost sight of the *intangibles*. He had forgotten (or never understood) that teams—and personal relationships—are built on more than practical skill. The intangibles, the communication, the respect offered in little ways, play such an important part.

In the basketball book that I wrote, called *Stuff! Good Players Should Know,* I included a special section on "Nodding to the Coach." I believed and still believe that a player can become much better, get along better, and get better instruction from the coach just by making it a habit to nod to the coach each time he or she offers some instruction or criticism.

Look away or ignore a teacher or coach, and soon that person will offer less to you. Nod—whether you happen to agree or not— in order to show you heard and understood, and you will continue to get that person's best effort. A coach will correct you and help you to learn fine points of the game that you never would have learned if you had made a point of tuning the coach out. The same goes for professors. Turn them into friends and they will help you to pass, to get scholarships, and to embark upon your career. Keep them at a distance and you will never even find out the many ways in which they may have been able to help you.

Teachers and professors are a great untapped resource which students constantly fail to take advantage of. Most of them are just a phone call away from the president of a company or the department head of a graduate school. Their position allows them to make a call to someone they don't even know to arrange an opportunity for you you never would have had. In most cases, especially if you have given something of yourself in order to turn them into friends, they will happily go out of their way to help, so seldom are they asked.

You may think intangibles shouldn't mean so much, but they are life itself. The so-called nuts and bolts, the actual class material or the actual sport, are in fact much less important.

No one, not even A students, can recall all the facts they memorized for exams down through the years. Few valedictorians could get even Bs on their sixth-grade history tests if they were forced to take them over without any review. Few would remember that Vasco da Gama sailed around the Cape of Good Hope, or that it was an eccentric named James W. Marshall who first discovered gold at Sutter's Mill in 1848.

But when you approach your professors and become the first student ever to ask what they wrote their dissertation on (the thing they slaved over for three to ten years of their lives), they will likely remember you and find you special.

Their books are jammed with papers,
covered with big ink blots and ugly doodles,
pages are torn out, and the binding coming apart.
Homework assignments are haphazardly folded,
looking more like half-finished paper airplanes . . . .

How to Keep Your Books
and Papers in Order

Some students will look at this title and think there is some definite order, a one-two-three kind of thing, that books should be in. First comes algebra or arithmetic, and zoology of course comes last, right? Nice and neat and always alphabetical!

No, of course not. By order, I mean the opposite of chaos. It is also the opposite of a lack of pride and concern.

Let me give just one example. The point is simple, but very important. By simply looking at the condition of the books and notebooks of many students, it is possible to see why they hate school and studying. Their books are jammed with papers, covered with big ink blots and ugly doodles, pages are torn out, and the binding is coming apart. Homework assignments are haphazardly folded, looking more like half-finished paper airplanes than like reports that actually have to be read by a teacher.

If you get in the habit of treating your books and papers like enemies—throwing them in your locker, dropping them in the dirt, and letting papers scatter in the wind—they *will* be like enemies.

Books and papers should be treated like your best friends, with kindness, gentleness, respect. Why? For the same reason anyone tends to pick up a new book rather than an old, dirty one. It is more enjoyable to spend time with a book that smells new, looks good, and is not so marked up that it is unreadable.

Why do successful business people carry expensive leather briefcases? Mostly to show their pride in the things they are carrying and working on.

Naturally, students don't need expensive leather briefcases. But a big brown file envelope with a firm piece of cardboard in it would do nicely to keep papers in order, unbent, and looking good without making your classmates think you have suddenly taken a job at IBM.

Put shiny new book covers on old books, and don't stuff any papers in them. Doing so just stretches the binding and encourages the book to come apart.

Organization of this type isn't something I am suggesting for the books' sake. What do I care about your books? You can burn them or toss them off the edge of a cliff for all I care. But if you plan to *use* a book, you ought to treat it well just so it is more fun to open it each day. Most people don't like having to work with books and papers that have curled edges and bad folds. Besides, you lose things more easily when they are tossed here and there and stuffed into a book or jammed in your locker.

Having papers in order and keeping clean, crisp book covers are not signs of prissiness. It is simply smart to stay organized, to know where things are, and to treat your papers and books with respect—*as though* you like them.

When I see a student drop a book and dozens of papers come pouring out and then get jammed back in, I *know* that student is hardly going to sit down with that same book in the evening and embark on an enjoyable mission of exploration and discovery. He or she doesn't even know how to *pretend* to like the book.

There is nothing wrong with pretending. Start pretending you like books, and it will be difficult not to care more. Just try it for a week. Put new covers on your books. Get that envelope with the stiff piece of cardboard, get some red sheets of paper, and neatly print the title of each of your subjects at the top. Most of you would be changed by this one-week effort, but you know what? Most of you will not be able to pull it off.

Weaklings.

*Everyone has had the experience of hearing an old song
and instantly recalling a person or event from the past.
The same applies to smells, sounds, colors, shapes, and so on.
The more you can bring into the memory process,
the better your chances of recalling the desired information.*

Test-Taking, Mural Making, and Study-Kits

For most students, it's no thrill to have to review dozens of pages of notes and hundreds of pages of text to study for a test. Even if you generally enjoy your courses, it is rarely fun learning and relearning material, and trying to memorize it well enough to be able to answer anything a professor might ask. As a result, studying can be tiresome or burdening, even for the best students.

There is no way to turn test-preparation into a Saturday afternoon picnic in the park, but there is a way to make it much easier and more effective. It involves what I call "mural-making" and the "study kit."

The Card-Catalog Effect

Remember, your mind works like a card catalog or computer, with dozens of cross-references. Therefore "red," for example, may be found under "colors" but also under "communism," "baseball," (Cincinnati Reds, Boston Red Sox), "reading materials" (stuff you *read*), or "blood." Obviously the list could go on. But you get the point.

Most everyone has had the experience of hearing an old song

and instantly recalling a person or event from the past. The same applies to smells, sounds, colors, shapes, and so on. The more you can bring into the memory process, the better your chances of recalling the desired information.

Not only is this creative process effective in the way it adds recall elements to your memory, but it also adds energy and interest to the preparation process itself.

Consider the difference between these two students. One trudges off to the library to pour over pages of notes and reading material, flipping page after page with a general sense of, "Oh no, I have to study." The second is creating something new, a collage of ideas, colors, shapes, and signs. This year's test could be next year's wallpaper! How? By using a study kit.

The Study Kit

A study kit is like an old-time doctor's little black bag. It contains all the things you need to help you study more effectively. What are some of those things?

Magic markers, many different colors
Pens, different colors
Colored paper
Scissors
Paper clips
Ruler
A drafting compass
Glue (stick form, please; no mess!)
Scotch tape
Paper (a roll of shelf paper if possible; if not, normal notebook
        paper, preferably without lines)

You can add anything you want, but the items above will certainly get you started.

Do yourself a favor and keep these items in some sort of case so that you don't have to look for them every time you want to prepare for a test.

Mural-Making

Once you have your kit assembled, you are ready. Get the material you need to know for the test in front of you, and start putting it down in mural form, on a large sheet of paper. If you can't afford big poster boards or shelf paper, then simply tape together four normal sized pieces of notebook paper. It's important to do a mural with nice *big* poster-sized paper in front of you. Although your brain works like a computer, *you* are not a micro chip. You cannot recall dozens of important facts if you write all of them down on the back of a postage stamp! Instead, you want to put them down on a large poster, *creatively.*

The word creatively is the key here. Each time you study for a test, the actual preparation becomes a test in itself.

How are you being tested? To see how imaginatively you can assemble on your mural all the things you need to know so that you cannot possibly forget them. It is a game, and the big question is, "Just how creative can I be? How can I make my job of recall easier?" Obviously, one way of trying to remember a group of facts is simply to read them over. A better way is to write them all down and repeat them out loud as you write them down. An even better way is to translate them into pictures, symbols, colors, anything that will aid your memory process.

Bananastands in Afghanistan

To make this clear, let's take an actual example.

Let's assume that your course is "Modern International Relations" and you are being tested on Russian-American relations since World War II. Initially, that may sound like a pretty dull subject to many students; therefore, the various aspects would be especially hard to recall a day later, with the book closed, and time ticking by during the test.

How would *you* recall a list of facts like these?

The building of the Berlin Wall.
The Cuban Missile Crisis.

The threat of nuclear war.

The invasion of Afghanistan.

The treatment of Soviet Jews.

The treatment of dissidents like Andrei Sakharov.

The defection of top ballet stars like Rudolf Nureyev and Mikhail Baryshnikov.

The U2 incident.

The boycott of the Olympic Games.

The Lithuanian sailor who jumped overboard.

The viewpoint of former presidential advisor Zbigniew Brzezinski.

The different methods of counting nuclear warheads.

The incarceration of reporter Nicholas Daniloff.

The United States' first-strike nuclear policy.

Gorbachev's glasnost.

Trying to remember all of these fifteen major points would be extremely difficult without gimmicks. But with gimmicks—with a map or drawing—it can be easy. Let's begin.

For the Berlin wall, draw a wall running through a circle and label the two sides East and West.

For the Cuban missile crisis, draw a big Cuban cigar standing straight up. Or put it in someone's mouth about to be spit up into the sky.

For the threat of nuclear war, draw a big mushroom cloud over your whole paper. That threat influences—hangs over—everything.

For the invasion of Afghanistan, draw a banana stand. Afghanistan banana stand. It's nonsense. But so what? Nonsense will be easy to recall the next day.

The Russian treatment of Soviet Jews could be drawn with a Star of David (a typical Jewish symbol) in the sky. The treatment of Russian dissident Sakharov might be drawn merely as a sack, or a sack of rope, SACK-a-rov—whatever it takes to help you to remember it.

Draw two ballet dancers to help you recall the defectors Nureyev and Baryshnikov.

The U2 incident involved a jet and pilot named Powers. So draw a *power*ful jet in the sky. The boycott of the Olympic Games might be drawn as a boy on a cot. The Lithuanian sailor might be drawn falling into the water.

Zbigniew Brzezinski's viewpoint, that U.S.-Soviet relations haven't changed much despite the public's alternating euphoria and fear, might be drawn with a big graph and two lines, one going straight across for his unchanging view, the other showing the public's high peaks and low valleys. You might label the graph "ZZ" to help you recall Zbigniew BrZeZinski's name.

You could draw an abacus to show the methods of counting nuclear warheads, or you could draw two little kids counting in the dirt. For the incarceration of writer Nicholas Daniloff you could draw a man behind bars. Show him with a pencil in his hand—or in his ear—whatever will make that picture more vivid to you.

For the Russian fear of our first-strike policy—our willingness to use nuclear weapons (which we demonstrated against Japan in World War II)—you might draw a baseball player swinging at a strike, or an umpire signaling "Strike one!" To make your picture more vivid, draw the umpire holding a Japanese flag, to help remind you that the Russians have a legitimate fear of our first-strike policy.

Do You Get the Picture?

You should realize from these fifteen examples that pictures are more vivid to your mind—and more easily recalled—than a group of words. But now, how are you going to remember all those pictures? Some may just jump out at you at test time—like the Cuban cigar, or the man behind bars, the banana stand, or the ZZ graph. But how do you make sure you can remember all of them? Easy. You string them together. Tie them together so that one automatically makes you remember the next. Let's start.

Attach the powerful U2 jet to the star of David in the sky. Draw some lines down to the sea, showing that the plane was shot down, and beside those lines show your dripping wet Lithuanian sailor. Have him dreaming of catching some Z's on a nice dry bed—a boy on a cot—so you get that Olympic tie-in; then have two ballet dancers looking at him on the cot. Both of course are smoking cigars and holding bananas. An umpire is telling them to get out. Or is it just a first strike he is calling?

Have that umpire sit on a (Berlin) wall, or perhaps with one leg on the wall and the other on a sack. If he has one finger pointing out one strike, have your little kids looking on with two and three fingers stretched out, bringing in that nuclear warhead counting method. Beside those two little kids is Daniloff, behind bars. A mushroom cloud hangs over the whole thing, and sitting on that cloud might very well be Gorbachev himself—with a glass nose signifying glasnost.

Does it sound difficult? It isn't. It's easy. It's even fun—or at least a helluva lot more interesting than pouring over pages of words. You create your own nonsense. Use numbers, shapes, arrows, lines, circles, trees, fences, monsters, clowns. Let your imagination soar. If it helps you to have Daniloff reaching through bars, with five Olympic rings on his fingers strangling a two-headed ballet dancer, do it. Draw it. You don't have to be Picasso to take advantage of pictures. It may help to use the ABCs (*A*fghanistan, *B*erlin, *C*uba, *D*aniloff . . .). Sometimes numbers will help (*one* strike, U-*two* jet, *three* bananas, *four* nuclear warheads, *five* Olympic rings . . .).

If one particular item doesn't seem to fit in your string, just draw a red circle around it. Or place it in a corner. Or draw a red apple and place a face or concept on it. The change of color, or the position on your paper is usually all your mind needs to recall it when you need it. Draw arrows; use colors, shapes, signs, whatever you can think of.

The great part is that, while others are becoming bored reading over line after line of words, your mind will be working, racing, grappling with how to turn facts into nonsense pictures that are impossible to forget. This effort changes the whole nature of the studying process, and it trains your mind to become better and better at making associations, creating pictures, and remembering facts.

During the actual test, your mind will be able to recall the shapes and colors easily, as well as the material associated with these things, *if* you have tied them together creatively. Another important by-product of this method is that each time you study for a test, you are actually stretching your mind and developing your creativity. Like anything else, practice brings improvement. You may find that at first you are not very good at translating book material into mural material. But after you have studied like this for a few months, you will find that you are quite good at it—and getting better all the time.

The difference between forcing material into your head, against your will, and feeling challenged to see just how creatively you can translate facts from book to mural is like night and day.

See for yourself.

As you go searching for the perfect answer,
make it a point to learn a couple of details
that even the professor is unlikely to know. . . .

How to "Cheat" Your Way to Success on Essay Tests

Most of you have already guessed that this book isn't likely to give you ways to *actually* cheat more effectively. We aren't really going to teach you new ways to stretch your neck or to see other people's answers all the way across a room!

But on essay tests, there are some methods that are so effective they almost ought to be called cheating. They work time and time again.

What Kind of Test Will It Be?

Before any test, it makes sense to ask your teacher or professor what kind of test you will have. If it is an essay test, find out how many questions will be on it. Nearly all teachers will be willing to give out this much information, and it can be very helpful in your test preparation.

Preparing Your Answers in Advance

Let's assume here that the professor has told you there will be just one essay question on your test. Here is how to prepare your answer in advance.

First, go through your notes and jot down just one idea—what you think is *the* most important idea—from each page. Then flip through your textbook or any other material pertinent to the course, and do the same thing, jotting down just one idea from every page.

This kind of studying is easy. It is browsing, it is effortless; yet it appeals to your mind and permits your mind to review and recall all sorts of information surrounding the facts that you jot down.

After you have finished jotting things down, look over everything and make a simple decision: If you were giving the test, what one question would you ask? Or, what one question can you think of that will permit you to demonstrate a significant amount of knowledge about the course?

Just Like an Open-Book Test

Good students, of course, will be better at anticipating these questions than poor students. In fact, good students sometimes are able to guess exactly right. But regardless of how well you guess, you now have something special going for you. You have a definite question to answer, and you can set out purposefully with the task of preparing the perfect answer—with your open book in front of you.

In other words, your studying is now carefully directed. You are searching your books and your notes with a purpose, and your mind responds actively, remembering much more of what you came across than it would if you were trying to force it to absorb facts with no aim or direction.

As you seek out the perfect answer, you are not making any effort to absorb anything. You are merely trying to assemble the information that will make up the perfect answer—and your relaxed mind will absorb and retain more in this process.

Add Some Impressive Details

As you go searching for the perfect answer, make it a point to learn precisely a couple of details that even the professor is unlikely to remember—exactly how many soldiers fought in the Battle of Gettysburg, for example. Or what the population of Philadelphia was when that city became the nation's capital.

What's the point of this extra detail? To impress the professor, nothing more.

Will it work?

Think about it.

Assigning Grades to Essay Tests

Imagine a professor trying to grade a group of thirty or forty essay tests. First of all, she is bored. She knows the answer better than anyone. She has read all about this subject. She has done her dissertation on it. She has heard experts speak about it. She has discussed these things and considered them from many angles. And now she has to read the hasty scribbles of a group of students, some of whom don't really care at all, many of whom are much more interested in the grade they get than in the material itself. How exciting can these papers be?

Add to the grading process some very real and usually unavoidable human factors—like that the professor's dog is scratching to go out, the kids are making noise, and the television is on. There are all sorts of possibilities. She may be thoroughly involved in her own research, thinking about moving, planning to write a book, or in a hurry for a meeting. Regardless of the circumstances, it will be difficult for her to give thirty similar answers her undivided, enthusiastic attention. No professor really enjoys grading papers. Nevertheless, it is something she must do.

Sure Cs for Students who Normally Flunk

The professor comes to some blank papers, or papers with just a few scribbles on them; these are marked easily with Fs. These students obviously don't know much about the topic.

Now what about *your* test paper? Let's assume that you didn't know the answer either. But your test paper is hardly blank, because you came prepared. You came to the class, having carefully prepared a good answer, containing all sorts of good information—even some special details—on some important aspects of the course material.

So, although you did not know the precise answer to the question, you made the best transition you could, and then you filled your paper with important material about the course.

Could the professor give *you* the same F she gave to the people who showed almost no knowledge of what was going on? Hardly. She would at least have to be impressed with your grasp of the information you did put down. If you could relate your material, in any way at all, to the actual question asked, your answer would have to look pretty good.

A Big Step Up for the Good Student

Now imagine the benefits of this method for students who are normally quite effective. They make excellent transitions to their well-prepared material, and include details and comparisons that no one else will use. In other words, they demonstrate not only knowledge of the material, but their ability to apply it, to compare and contrast it with other material.

Use the Answer You Prepare!

It should already be clear that, regardless of what the essay question is, you need to use the material you have prepared. The smarter you are, the better you will be at this. But in any case, the organization and preparation you have done in advance with an open book will nearly always enable you to raise your grade at least one notch, and often two.

A Three-Question Test

It should also be obvious to you that, if the professor has told you that you will have three essay questions, then the intelligent thing to do is to prepare three perfect answers—and make sure that all of your excellent, prepared material ends up on your test paper.

The only purpose of a test is to give students the opportunity to demonstrate that they have knowledge of the course. By preparing good answers in advance, you will enable yourself to demonstrate significant knowledge *every* time. Naturally, some of your prepared answers will fit better than others. But you will always be demonstrating an impressive grasp of some important information in the course.

No professor can discount that entirely—especially in relation to blank papers that have demonstrated nothing.

How to Prepare Answers—And Remember Them

Once you choose the information you want in your prepared answer, map it out; that is, draw it and employ gimmicks that will aid your memory. As we learned in the previous chapter, drawing a mural can be very effective in helping you to remember facts. This is especially true for essay questions, because the mural will help you to remember things in a logical sequence.

Furthermore, once you have prepared your mural, you will be relaxed at test time. While others are frantic, searching for answers, you will be busy demonstrating knowledge.

This method will pay dividends over and over again, so well that it's almost like cheating—only better. You can never get caught!

*Fun-to-study notes
are those that have pictures
drawn beside them. . . .*

How to Take Notes

Most people make one big mistake when taking notes. They take too many. They spend so much time writing, they don't really listen. They don't pick up the teacher's or professor's points of analysis, and they don't get a chance to add their own thoughts to the ideas being presented.

The art of taking good notes involves two other "arts" not often considered by students: (1) the art of taking notes that are easy—and fun—to study and recall, and (2) the art of listening.

Fun Notes

Fun-to-study notes are those that have pictures drawn beside them, that have "editorial" comments here and there, and that are brief and clear. The purpose of notes is simply to remind you of something.

So, take fewer notes, and start trying to fill the paper with things that will not only remind you of the material you need to know, but that also will be interesting to refer to.

If you make an effort to do this, you will get better and better at it. But if your idea of note-taking is just to furiously copy down every word the professor says, you may never get better at anything except having more to study.

Good Listening

To listen well and pay proper respect to the speaker, you can't have your eyes constantly on the paper in front of you. Your eyes need to be on the speaker about 80 percent of the time. In other words, most of the time you should listen, watch, and think, occasionally jotting something down.

Try it. It is not only easier, it's better for you!

If you come to some questions that you just don't understand, don't get discouraged. They may be the ones that don't count. Just go on and get as many right answers as you can.

The SAT: Just Another Test

These books on how to "crack" the Scholastic Aptitude Test (SAT), or how to improve your scores by hundreds of points, always amuse me. You can't crack the SAT any more than you can suddenly become a movie star. If you haven't read a book or magazine in the past three years, you are not going to score well on the vocabulary section, regardless of what tips you get out of some save-the-day kind of course or book.

There are, however, a few things you should know that take some of the mystery and pressure away.

First, SATs are a lot of hubbub about nothing. All sorts of successful people had low SAT scores—and many people with high SAT scores have been failures in college, in life, in all sorts of things. But you have to understand that the SAT is just one means of placing a standard on students. It isn't nearly as important as people think.

It is true that a low score may keep you from going to the "college of your choice." But what is the big deal about the college of your choice? What is that choice based on? Few high-school students have any idea where they will be happiest. You might look at a brochure, walk around the campus, hear something that someone said. But you don't *know* where you will be happiest. Only one thing is certain: You *can* be happy at *any* college in the United States.

Colleges are not prisons; they can be great places. In any school you can find a niche where you can blossom and grow.

So you get low SAT scores and you can't go to the college of your choice. Big deal. So you have to go somewhere else for a couple of years. Do well and transfer if it still means that much to you. Chances are it won't; but if it does, transferring is no big thing.

Some Questions Aren't Even Scored

You can do well on the SATs with a lot of sleep or with no sleep. Naturally, if you stay awake for three nights in a row, it may be hard to think or even to read on the day of the exam. Don't get so worked up that you can't sleep on the night before the test, but if you do, don't worry; sleep isn't that crucial. When you sit down to take the exam, your adrenalin will take over. You will be alert enough to answer the questions you can answer. The SAT isn't that different from any other test. You have some questions and some possible answers, and you have to think, recall what you know, and solve some problems. And unless you are very rare, you will get some questions right and miss others.

Another thing you should know is that some SAT questions are experimental; they are of interest to the test-makers but do not count on your total score. So, if you come to some questions that you just don't understand, don't get discouraged. They may be the ones that don't count. Just go on and get as many right answers as you can.

If you haven't finished a section, and the test supervisor says to stop, don't worry. Many people who don't finish the exam still do well. I know this from personal experience. I was no "brain," but I managed a combined score of nearly 1300; and I don't think I finished *any* of the sections. Don't worry when others seem to finish quickly and seem totally relaxed. They are often the ones who just mark down answers thoughtlessly because they have become discouraged and have stopped trying. The students with the best scores are usually working hard until the end of the exam period; if they have finished, they often check their answers or return to the "tough" questions that they left blank the first time through.

Cheating

You cannot cheat.

My brother had a friend of limited academic skills who walked out of his SAT and confidently told my brother he was sure he had scored highly. My brother doubted him instantly, yet was surprised by his confidence since it manifested itself in a realm in which he was not typically given to boasting.

"What makes you think you got a higher score?" my brother asked.

"I copied all your answers," the kid said. "But I read over this one and happened to know the answer to it—and it was different from your answer. I would've told you, but you looked busy the whole time, and I figure it wouldn't look good if we had *all* the same answers anyway!"

There was just one problem. The kid had all the same answers, but he didn't realize that his test finished with a math section, whereas my brother's finished with a verbal! Obviously, he didn't have the same answers at all. He didn't realize that the people in Princeton who make that test aren't suckers. They mix the test questions around. It's no big deal. Computers can do that with no problem—and correct the papers too. As a result, the people sitting near you will never have the same order of questions as you. That is why the procedure for administering the test is so strict—to make it impossible for conventional methods of cheating to be successful. Nothing is left to chance. If you go into the SAT planning to copy from someone, you have no chance to succeed. Period.

Obviously, I have no interest in trying to convince you of your moral "duty" to do your own work. I am simply saying that since you have no other choice, you may as well just sit there, do your best, and see what happens.

Take the SAT Early

Don't wait until your senior year. If you dislike exams, naturally your tendency will be to put off taking the SAT until you absolutely must do it. But in this case you must overcome your tendency to procrastinate, because you should find out as soon as possible what your situation is going to be, so you can plan accordingly. It doesn't make sense to go all the way through high school planning on going to Harvard and then finding that your SAT scores are low. Your plans will make a lot more sense if you have an idea of the possibilities. If you take the SAT in your sophomore year and get a combined score of 800, you can reasonably expect to be in the 900 to 1000 range by senior year. But few people vastly increase their score, so taking the test early will give you a sense of where you are, and what schools will be likely to consider your application seriously. That way, you can concentrate on realistic possibilities. Why fool yourself?

Preparation Courses

If you have the money to take an SAT preparation course, go ahead. It certainly can't hurt, and it is likely to help somewhat. If nothing else, such a course will familiarize you with the process, so you'll be a good deal less nervous when you take the exam. Also, your ability to concentrate will be enhanced since you will know exactly what to expect.

On the other hand, if you simply take the test early in your high-school career, you can relax, knowing that there is time to improve. The pressure will be off, and you can learn what it's all about by actually doing it.

Essentially, the SAT is composed of two sections. The verbal section tests your knowledge of vocabulary, your ability to read and answer questions, and your ability to recognize good grammar. The math section includes word problems and various kinds of calculations that test your ability to use basic mathematical concepts. All of the questions have multiple-choice answers; you simply mark down the best choice among the five offered. It sounds easy, but of course, the test-makers try to make all the possible answers look reasonable.

How do you score well on the SAT? The best way is to have parents who read you stories at night before you went to bed, who took you to the library once a week when you were growing up, and who made reading a fun family project. If you had a mother or father who helped you learn the multiplication tables, or who bought you puzzles and educational toys, so much the better. If anything, the SAT measures the advantages you had while growing up.

If you *didn't* have parents like this, and didn't work extra hard in school to give yourself the same advantage as those who did, you may not do as well on the SAT. That does not mean you are doomed for life. It just means that you are not likely to be able to do well on the skills the SAT measures. You cannot develop a good vocabulary with willpower and determination. Over the next ten years you can, but not over the next ten months—not with all the other school work you have to do in that same period of time.

What's the point of all this explanation? In my opinion, it is simply this: *relax.* Regardless of how you do, there are options. There are colleges that only accept students with high SAT scores. But there are many fine schools, where you can get a good education, that accept students "conditionally," or that accept students with lower scores. Besides, if you do well during your first two years of college, you can transfer. So, ultimately, your success or failure in life is not going to depend on how well you do on the SAT.

At most, the SAT will have some influence on where you spend your nineteenth and twentieth years of life. Those should be years of growth, struggles, and good times, no matter where you are. So cheer up. If you have a good date on the night before the SAT tests, don't cancel it. Enjoy it. Just try to come home at a decent hour, so you can stay awake the next morning! Really. It ain't no big deal. Don't let 'em fool you.

"The play's the thing!"
—Shakespeare.

A Word On Book Reports

It seems as though I wrote a million book reports during my school days. Students still have to do them, and often they have considerable difficulty. Therefore, I have one brief suggestion:

If possible, choose a play. Not many students choose to write about plays, but doing so makes a great deal of sense because plays are always short! Think about it. Plays are performed on stage. How many people have time to go to six-hour plays? Not many. So playwrights write plays that take a couple of hours, maybe less, to perform—and that even counts changing props and altering the stage, opening and closing curtains, applause, and so on; if a play can be seen in two hours, it can be read in an hour and a half even by slow readers. That means you can read the entire play, pull out some memorable passages here and there, and explain the major gimmick (almost every play has a major gimmick or method) that helps the writer to make his or her points and present the story.

If you follow the basic format for writing papers, you can come up with a pretty good report in a few hours or so. And you don't even need Cliff Notes!

Quotations give your paper life.
Keep your own opinions brief, and let the stars speak for you.
It will take the focus off your efforts
and keep it on those who write for a living!

How to Write a Paper

In the course of your high school and college studies, you will likely be required to write a number of papers. Many people go to great lengths to avoid the classes in which professors assign papers. I clearly recall some very intelligent students at Duke University saying, "Don't take that class—you'll have to write three papers."

In my opinion, the classes with the papers were the easiest. Papers are essentially open-book, no-pressure exams. Your task in a paper is to demonstrate knowledge, and to show that your mind has worked; you have to compare and contrast some things, and give examples to back up your opinions. That's all there is to it. A paper is like a test in which you are permitted to skip the parts you don't know. It does not require that you do one particular thing, it merely requires that you do *some*thing.

Currently I am reading two books, so I will use them to illustrate. *Shoeless Joe,* by W. P. Kinsella, is about a baseball fanatic who builds a ball park on his Iowa farm in response to a mysterious "voice" that initially only he can hear.

Love in the Time of Cholera was written by Gabriel Garcia Marquez, one of the most renowned authors in the history of Spanish literature. The book explores love, particularly the determined, fanatical love of Florentino Ariza, who sees a woman one day and decides on the spot that he is in love with her. He carries that love with him throughout his entire life, though she never gives him the time of day.

Now, suppose I had to write a paper comparing these two books. For some, this seems like an impossible task. But it is actually quite easy. The key is to let better writers do your work for you. All you need to do is supply the format. Think of it as a banquet. You are merely the master of ceremonies. You introduce the speakers, and let them do the clever talking. So you introduce the two books, as I have just done, and let the authors go from there. You don't have to do the work. You don't have to come up with amazing thoughts. Let the authors speak for themselves.

You can use the same basic format or process over and over again. Begin with a general summary of the two books or ideas you are dealing with. Then let the authors "argue." In other words, use a lot of quotes directly from the two books.

What should the quotes pertain to? To whatever questions you can think of that may be of interest to someone who never read either book. Don't be intimidated just because the teacher knows the two books better than you do. Write the paper as though it is being done for someone who has never heard of either book or author.

So, what kind of questions can be asked and then answered by the authors? Make a list before you begin. Here are some that could be asked about the two books I am reading:

How do these authors get us to believe in the strange situations they have set up?

What is particularly interesting about each book?

What stylistic quirks does each auther have?

What parts, do you think, was the author most happy with?

Why did these authors write these books? It takes a long time to sit down and write, and usually rewrite, a book. So, although the book may be dull to you, it took the author a great deal of time and effort. Therefore, regardless of what *you* think of a book, you ought to ask yourself: Why would this author have put so much time and effort into this? What was he or she really hoping to get across?

Once you have asked and answered some questions like these,

you should decide how you want to string this information together so that it seems continuous, not like a bunch of ideas just thrown together. You don't have to be particularly worried about the proper order of things. There is no proper order of things. But if you find two or three stylistic quirks, for example, write about them in the same paragraph, rather than noting one and then mentioning another two pages later. When you're talking to a friend, it's all right to interrupt and say, "Oh yeah, I remember what it was I wanted to tell you yesterday." In a paper, though, you need to be more organized.

So, choose an order—just be careful to group similar things together. If you can't find any similarities, fine. It's okay to begin by saying there are five points of particular interest in comparing the two books and then explain each point in a separate section.

Remember, create the skeleton, and let the authors do the talking. Here's an example:

> The two authors have different ways of telling a story. Kinsella is breezy, as though he is standing with you on a street corner, telling stories, throwing in interesting facts here and there. Marquez seems to delight in description. When he tells you something, he wants you to feel it completely, to be absorbed in it.
>
> Look at two contrasting descriptions about a restless night. First Kinsella: "I have been more restless than usual this night."
>
> Now Marquez:

> Dr. Juvenal Urbino did not sleep at all on the night of his return; he was frightened by the darkness and silence, and he said three rosaries to the Holy Spirit and all the prayers he could remember to ward off calamities and shipwrecks and all manner of night terrors, while a curlew that had come in through a half-closed door sang every hour on the hour in his bedroom. He was tormented by the hallucinating screams of the mad women in the Divine Shepardess Asylum next door, the harsh dripping from the water jar into the wash basin which resonated throughout the house, the long-legged steps of the curlew wandering in his bedroom, his congenital fear of the dark, and the invisible presence of his dead father in the vast, sleepless mansion. . . .

> *That* is sleeplessness!

Was I comparing apples with oranges? That's not so bad. Some of your comparisons may not be perfect. The authors were not writing with each other in mind. But if you read two books and think for a few moments, there will always be some similarities, some differences, some ways to compare and contrast the authors' methods of telling their stories.

Quotations give your paper life. Keep your own opinions brief, and let the stars speak for you. Let curlews wander in bedrooms with dead fathers' ghosts and let the screams of mad women into *your* paper. It will take the focus away from your efforts and keep it on those who write for a living!

In a nutshell, lay out a general summary at the beginning. Answer a list of questions in an orderly manner, letting the material speak for itself, comparing and contrasting constantly and making sure you give examples for every claim you make. Don't say anything unless you back it up with evidence. Imagine that everything you say is being heard by some argumentative little brat who says, "Prove it!" every few seconds. Finally, conclude with a brief statement that doesn't do much more than repeat your general thesis.

Perhaps most important of all, don't keep putting off a paper, allowing it to seem more and more difficult. You are not going to get much smarter in a week. So just follow the formula. Summarize. Make a list of questions. Browse over your answers. Group whatever you can and decide on an order. And then go to it, letting the material speak for itself.

Like anything else, the more you do it, the easier it will get.

Oh yeah, and now I remember what I wanted to tell you yesterday! Even though you may think that comparing *Love in the Time of Cholera* with *Shoeless Joe* is a waste of time, it actually will help you learn to think, forcing your mind to work—and develop. Pushups and jogging are not everyone's idea of fun either, but they are what make touchdowns and home runs possible.

Happy conditioning!

If you just grapple and keep at it,
it becomes like tying a shoe or riding a bike.
Just minutes before five-year-olds figure out how to tie a shoe,
they cannot do it. Think about that.

How to Succeed in College

There are a lot of ways to succeed or to make the most of your college experience, and of course, everyone has a different definition of what success is. But this section deals with the primary concern of most high-school students: Will I be able to pass? Will I flunk out? Will the work be too hard? Will I be able to make it?

These questions *are* the primary consideration; obviously, if you flunk out, nothing else about success matters. Perhaps you have a blueprint for how to meet people, how to have a good time, how to build a business while you are a student. But none of that will matter if you flunk out. So let's get back to what it takes *not* to flunk out. Better yet, let's explore the reason why students flunk out, as soon as we discuss a few of the typical student's concerns.

Worries

Many students go off to college worried that they will not be bright enough, that the course work will be too demanding, that they just won't understand the material or have the time to get all the work done.

These fears are unnecesssary. Anyone who goes to college and *tries* will succeed, even students who are not very bright at all. Professors are usually incredibly compassionate, sympathetic, and helpful. If you talk to them and tell them you are having trouble *early* in the course (not a day before the final test, after you have accumulated a string of flunking grades), they will help you. They will see to it that you succeed, either by giving you hints about what may be on the test, or by assigning you extra work. Very few professors will let you flunk their courses if you show them from the beginning that you are sincerely trying.

The Failure Pattern

So how does anyone fail? Simple. The pattern repeats itself over and over again. It goes roughly like this:

You attend a class and you aren't exactly excited by the material, or you don't understand it very well. The professor assigns some reading, and since you don't like "that stuff" very much, or because you don't understand it, you don't do it. You go to the next class, and you can't follow the lecture very well, and don't participate in the classroom discussion of the material because you haven't done the reading.

The plot thickens—and the pattern continues. You don't listen very well in class because you don't understand. You don't do the reading because you need to have the material explained to you. You figure, "No use spending valuable time reading this stuff I don't understand. Better to use my time on stuff I do understand."

So you stop doing the assignments and paying attention in class. Eventually you stop going to class.

"No use wasting my time going to class—I don't understand this stuff anyway," you rationalize. And the class is useless if you haven't read the material. "I'm better off staying in the library and reading the material on my own."

Maybe. But do you go to the library and read the material?

In a short time, you have justified not going to class and not reading the material—all because, at the beginning, you did not quite understand, or you soon decided that you didn't like the course.

I hope you can see the fallacy of such a pattern, and instead will commit yourself to grappling. That's right, grappling. Go the first day and listen. Do the assignments. If you don't understand, try. Go to class and try to participate. If you mess up or say something "stupid," so what? It is a lot more intelligent to try and to sometimes say something stupid, than to drop out.

Few people, even those who may chuckle at your attempt to participate, will actually find you stupid for trying. So you don't know everything. Big deal. Try. Go to class. Read the assignments. Ask questions. Talk to the professor.

Stay involved. Stay active. Grapple.

If you do these things, you will succeed in college, even if your SAT scores were low and you didn't do particularly well in high school. You may not get all As, but you *will* get through.

If you can get good grades, that's terrific. If you can demonstrate to those around you that you can do superior work regardless of what course or professor is thrown at you, wonderful. More power to you. You are surely going to succeed, and you deserve the congratulations and the honors that will come to you.

But if you have to struggle just to pass, struggle. You may not win awards or impress everyone with your quick grasp, but so what? What kind of person would you like to have operating on your heart? The "brain" who never studied? Or the somewhat-less-intelligent but very diligent person who took whatever time was necessary to make sure he or she knew the stuff? Sure, you would *like* to think that *your* doctor is both very bright and very diligent. Me too! But given a choice, I would want the person who may not have been the brightest, but who was diligent and hardworking—and determined to learn everything necessary to operate successfully.

If you go to college with the idea of grappling, of going after knowledge and staying involved until you get it, you will succeed. If you allow yourself in the beginning to base your actions on whether or not you like things, whether or not to go to class, and whether or not to pay close attention, you will quickly fall into the failure pattern.

If you just grapple and keep at it, it becomes like tying a shoe or riding a bike. Just minutes before five-year-olds figure out how to tie a shoe, they cannot do it. Think about that. They do not appear to be getting better at *almost* tying shoes. Usually they simply cannot get it—then suddenly, they can!

Course work is the same way. Sometimes you can go for several weeks not understanding; then suddenly, it starts to make sense. Pieces of the puzzle begin to fit, and the whole picture begins to make sense. You just have to keep after it. The puzzle won't present itself while you are rationalizing and making excuses. It will present itself while you are trying to make it make sense.

Good luck.

Good luck? No, let me take that back. You won't need luck, if you have already committed yourself to trying. Show me someone who has flunked out of college, and I'll show you someone who stopped trying to make it. It's that simple.

3

Potpourri:
How to Do All Sorts of Things

Regardless of where you go,
you will need to carve out your own niche
and become involved using your own initiative.

How to Choose a Good College

The question of choosing a good college reminds me of an old elephant joke.

How do you find an elephant?

You don't have to. Elephants are so big they hardly ever get lost!

Choosing a good college is easy. It shouldn't even be a subject in this book at all, except that many students and parents are concerned about it. So. . . .

First, it is impossible to choose a *bad* college. Next time you hear people talk about getting into a good college, ask them to make you a list of bad colleges. A list of bad colleges will be very hard to come by. The bad ones nearly all went out of business years ago.

Of course, someone can always rent a building, put up a sign that says Joe's Business College, and rip off everyone in sight. But Joe's Business College will not appear in a typical college directory.

Therefore, if you want to be sure to choose a good college, simply go to your bookstore or library and get a college directory. It will list colleges all over the nation.

Of course, you have to determine your own needs. Do you want to live right in a big, bustling city, or on a self-contained campus, with dorms, library, cafeteria, and classrooms all in sight of one another?

Do you need the flexibility that a big school offers, with a much broader course of study and many more alternatives? Do you want a place where you are anonymous, or a place where "everyone knows everyone"? There are advantages to both, of course; it just depends on your preferences.

Which colleges offer what you want to study? If you want to attend a large state university, it doesn't much matter what you want to study; the university will have it, or at least have something that leads you in the right direction. But if you are considering a small school, you must make sure it offers a course of study that appeals to you.

Finding Your Niche

Regardless of where you go, you will need to carve out your own niche and become involved using your own initiative. Whether your extracurricular activities include student government, the school paper, activist groups, drama, dance, or sports, the choice is up to you.

Read any college's general bulletin or brochure and you will find a wide variety of options and alternatives under "Student Life" or some such heading. Nearly every college offers abundant opportunity.

College, after all, is not prison. It is a wonderful opportunity to learn, grow, and become yourself fully as you prepare for a future career.

Every college has a dedicated president and a board of trustees who are trying to improve the total educational experience, and professors who have given virtually their whole lives to the study of science, history, or mathematics and who have much to share with you—if you want it.

Every college also has a variety of people—rich and poor, young and old, dedicated and drifting. It's all there. Life. But if you sit back and wait for the college to educate you and prepare you for the future, you will be disappointed. In that regard, even Harvard, Michigan, Stanford, and Duke will all fail you, literally and figuratively. However, if you are seeking knowledge, experience, and the expansion of your mind, it will be impossible to avoid gaining those things, regardless of where you go.

Flip through a directory. On one page alone you will find La

Verne, Lawrence, Lebanon Valley, Lee, Lehman, LeMoyne, Lenoir-Rhyne, LeTourneau, and Lewis.

We just raced through California, Wisconsin, Pennsylvania, Tennessee, New York, North Carolina, Texas, and Illinois. Most people have never heard of any of these schools; yet at any one of them you would find dozens of students in one day who would tell you how much they love their school. Each one offers interesting courses, interesting people, a chance to grow.

It really doesn't make much sense getting anxious about choosing a college. It is, fortunately, one of those rare times in life when it is nearly impossible to make a mistake.

If you are determined to hate a place, then even the best school will make you miserable. But if you go to college determined to get what you can from it, you will be hard-pressed *not* to enjoy it immensely.

If only all decisions were as fraught with success as that of choosing a college!

You cannot decide, after loafing through high school,
that you simply must attend Harvard.
On the other hand, even if you have
loafed through high school, that does not mean
you cannot someday end up with a Harvard degree.

How to Get Into College

Getting into the college of your choice is a completely different matter. Many schools have rigid admissions standards; for these you need a certain class rank or grade point average and high SAT or ACT scores. If you don't have the grades and scores required, you could stand on your head and whistle out your ears while reciting Shakespeare's sonnets, and you still wouldn't get in.

Do you believe it?

I'm pretty sure there is no particular demand for a Shakespeare scholar/headstanding ear-whistler at the school of your choice. You would stand a better chance if you wrote letters to and visited the right people.

Who are the right people? The president, the director of admissions, a professor you read about, or a rich alumnus who just happens to like you.

In other words, most schools do not have hard and fast admissions requirements. If you are dead-set on attending Harvard University, apply. If you get turned down, write or call the Admissions Office and ask what you would have needed to be admitted. If all you need is a few better grades, perhaps you can attend prep school for a year, to bring your grades up and add some advanced course work to your record. If you need higher test scores, you could study and prepare and then take the tests again.

Where there's a will, there's a way. You could always move to Cambridge, Massachusetts, and just sit in on some classes; tell the professor that you are having some difficulties with the registrar's office, but that you expect everything to be worked out, so if it's okay, you will attend the class until you get a definite yes or no. Mumble something about the bureaucracy, and the professor will understand.

If you are a bright, eager student, the professor will probably not care too much whether you are actually enrolled.

If you finish a class or two like that—with As—the Admissions Office may give your application more consideration next time; and certainly the admissions people will admire your spunk as well as your demonstrated ability.

There are many stories of students figuring out creative ways to gain admittance. One student tried and was refused three times by Columbia's prestigious School of Journalism. He wrote a book that became a bestseller and the next year he was invited to *teach* at the school!

Of course, this is an unusual case; but many students go to great lengths to get into the college or university of their choice. Is it all worth it? Is any school so crucial to your well-being and development that you should resort to outlandish means in order to get in? I think not. There are plenty of fine schools out there that present a whole range of possibilities. If one school won't let you in, go to another. How do you know which is best? That's like saying, at age eighteen, that you know for sure that one particular person will make a better spouse—at fifty—than anyone else. No one can be sure of such a thing, and the divorce rates are stark evidence of that.

If, however, there is just one school for you, then go there. Do whatever outlandish thing is necessary to get in. Gather the necessary information, find out what is required, get a list of rich alumni, make friends with the school's most famous professor, or ear-whistle until you are admitted.

But why get so worked up about getting into a particular school? If you cannot get into Harvard initially, you could go to Lawrence, or LeMoyne, or Lebanon Valley. Then, all you have to do is pull some good grades there, impress your professors as a dynamic individual and student, and transfer after two years. Or simply apply to a Harvard graduate school.

In summary, getting into a school is easy—if you meet the published requirements. If you do not, you have to decide just how much it means to you to attend that school, and explore some other methods of gaining admittance. In most cases, the best thing you can do is simply to choose to attend a school where you do meet the requirements, and then try to do well there. Demonstrate your worthiness where you are, and you will be ready when the time comes to take the next step.

You cannot decide, after loafing through high school, that you simply must attend Harvard. On the other hand, even if you have loafed through high school, that does not mean you cannot someday end up with a Harvard degree. Anything is possible. It will just take some extra planning, some extra effort, and no doubt some extra time—you just have to decide if it really is that important to you.

In most cases, the thing to do is to choose a school whose size, campus environment, course offerings, and admissions requirements match your needs and abilities. Go there and do well, enjoy it, and make the most of the total experience. Wear tee-shirts with your school's name on it. Carry notebooks with your school's colors. Send your family and friends a poster of your school's mascot. In other words, adopt the place. Make it yours completely. If it doesn't have the reputation of a Yale or an MIT, then spread the word to everyone you know about what a great place it is. Improve its reputation yourself!

And most of all, enjoy it. Live it, love it, and don't hurry through just to get it over with. College, as my brother always says, is the best six years of your life!

*Success is easy when you know exactly what you want to do
and you have had many years to do it.
Nevertheless, the majority of the successful people
have followed a much different pattern.*

How to Choose a Career—
And Get a Successful Start

It's not unusual for students approaching the end of high school to be anxious about the idea of a career; they don't even know what college major to take, let alone what they want to be.

They could flip through dozens of books on careers, visit hundreds of people, and ask thousands of questions about this and that job or. . . .

They could just relax and forget about it!

Don't Choose a Career, Let a Career Choose You

Probably the best thing you can do, if you don't know what you want to be, is to decide nothing. In the first couple of years of college, you can take a whole array of general courses: psychology, sociology, history, political science, mathematics, biology, music, art, and so on.

The list of possibilities is endless, and there is no danger in learning too much. Regardless of what you eventually choose to do, it will be worthwhile to have explored a wide variety of courses and ideas. In that sense, no effort—fortunately—is ever wasted. You will never know how an idea from one course may have a special influence on you later.

The mind is a grand synthesizer, constantly gathering bits and pieces of information in new patterns and pursuits.

Imagine any simple two-part tool; a hammer, for example. It was just a piece of iron and a piece of wood until someone got the idea to join them—and unleash a lot of power, not just in the physical abilities of the wood and iron, but in the imagination of anyone who uses them. Suddenly new ideas open up. The iron is shaped and a hammer is born.

On a more complex level, this same process goes on every day in the minds of entrepreneurs all over the world. People are constantly finding new uses for computers, new ways to apply software. But it is not just a matter of great technological advances, but of synthesizing what is already at hand.

Knowledge—even that which seems totally removed from everything else you are doing—may have dramatic consequences in your brain, and you may never even know it.

So regardless of what courses you take, you are not wasting time. You are building a broader foundation, a resource from which to draw for the rest of your life. In fact, every course you take that does *not* directly relate to your future profession gives you even more of an edge.

New ideas and sudden breakthroughs don't just come out of thin air. They are the result of the mind constantly going over all the information stored in it and putting together pieces of a puzzle in order to solve the current problem being grappled with.

It is not necessary for you to choose a career; ultimately, it will choose you. Simply take a variety of courses and relax, knowing that you are laying the groundwork for your future success—even though you have no idea what shape it may take.

Almost anyone will tell you how important it is to do the things you like. Your work is a big part of your life, so make sure you enjoy it. If your family is urging you to be a doctor, but you really prefer painting, then don't be afraid to become an artist. The people who truly care about you will always tell you to pursue what makes *you* happiest.

Some successful people have known exactly what they wanted to do by the time they were seven or eight years old. They are fortunate, because success is easy when you know exactly what you want to do and you have had many years to prepare for it. But the majority of successful people have followed a much different pattern. They started out in one field, changed to another, maybe changed again, tried other things. Most people have to try a lot of different directions before settling on the one thing that is right for them. Why should you be any different?

If you know exactly what you want, fine. Go for it. But if you don't, relax. Start down a path, and don't be afraid to veer off.

If you commit yourself to taking on each new venture with enthusiasm and dedication, impressing those around you with your energy and commitment, the world will open up for you. Opportunities will present themselves continually.

Your problem will never be having nothing to do; it will be having to sort out and reject many promising possibilities. That's not such a bad position to be in.

So relax. Fill your days with effort and enthusiasm for whatever you are doing. The rest will take care of itself. Take your career books back to the library. Chances are there isn't a book yet written about what you will be doing. The world is changing fast, and new opportunities are constantly out there for anyone willing to grasp them.

Something as subjective and complex
as getting a team to gel and work together
requires cohesion and communication. These qualities
are actually more important than talent or ability.

How to Make a Team—
Or Get Reinstated If You Get Dropped

Skeptics will look at this chapter title and think right away, "That's ridiculous. This guy can't tell anyone how to make a team. If he's so good, why doesn't he play for the Boston Celtics?"

They have a point. No one can tell you how to make any team under any circumstances. In my case with the Celtics, there is simply too large a gap in ability between me and those on the team. However, in cases when the gap is narrower, it is important to know how to give yourself every possible advantage. I have seen so many young and talented athletes sabotage their chances with bad attitudes. Often, these were kids who had enough skill to make the team.

Let me give another example of a guy planning to try out for a basketball team. "Are you working out with the guys during the summer?" I asked, assuming he would know that the players on the previous year's team work out together in the summer, often under the watchful eye of their coach.

The would-be player told me he was not working out with them. Yes, they were working out together, but he was planning to surprise the coach with how good he had gotten on his own!

While I liked his idea of getting good on his own, and the idea of surprising the coach, in this case it was simply foolish. During the summer a coach usually sizes up talent and makes plans for the upcoming season. And, in a team sport like basketball, it is important for a player to blend in with the others and to understand what the coach wants. Not practicing with the team and having the opportunity to learn what the coach was looking for hurt that player's chances considerably. Which brings me to the somewhat obvious focus of this chapter.

To give yourself the best possible chance to make a team, make sure you communicate well and often with the one who chooses the team.

I have heard many young athletes object, saying, "I'm not going to kiss his or her butt, or try to talk my way onto the team like so-and-so." My answer to that is simple: You *should* try to talk your way onto the team. It's a fact: Success is an combination of butt-kicking and butt-kissing.

Try to become the coach's "favorite."

Favoritism is an integral part of any endeavor. If I am choosing a team, why should I choose a bunch of guys I don't like and can't work with? Why shouldn't coaches choose their favorite players?

If you think you can boil life down to precise ability and statistics, you need a whole new course in Life 101. Something as subjective and complex as getting a group of people to gel and work together requires cohesion and communication. These qualities can actually be *more* important than talent or ability.

Traveling and practicing with a team during a long season can be a real ordeal, fraught with tension and ill feeling—if you let it become that. Therefore, knowing in advance that there will be some tough times, disappointing losses, criticism, personality conflicts, and so on, you want to at least begin the season with players who can get along, work together, and communicate with one another during good times. Otherwise, you will have little to build on in order to withstand the tough times.

The familiar accusations hurled at coaches by players dropped from a squad—"You play favorites" and "I can play better than so-and-so"—only confirm that cutting that player from the team was a good decision.

Getting Reinstated

If you've been cut from the squad, but want with all your heart to be on it, you might approach the coach with something like this:

"Coach, I understand why I got cut. I'm not as talented as some of the others, and I simply did not demonstrate that I can help this team win games this year. But I want to ask if there is some way you can give me an opportunity to change your mind. I am willing to work harder than anyone; I am willing to encourage the others and make sure that team morale stays high; I am willing to practice hard every day to push the others and make them better, without ever complaining about not getting a chance to play in the games. I will carry the water bucket, sweep the floors, do anything you ask, for an opportunity to be a part of this team."

Can you imagine saying *that* to a coach? Can you imagine the coach turning down a player with that kind of attitude?

Even if he or she says, "I'm sorry; I just don't have any more uniforms," you might follow with, "I'll just help in practice then," or, "What can I do to help you do *your* job better?"

These kinds of offers are compelling. Not what can *you* do for *me,* but what can *I* do for *you?*

Demonstrating an attitude like this, when others are grumbling, accusing, and sulking, can often get you reinstated or at least get you into some peripheral role from which you may later move into the center of things after someone gets hurt or quits, or after you have a chance to prove your worth. Extra uniforms have been known to just appear out of the sky when the situation warrants it.

Favoritism Reconsidered

Let's look once more at this whole business of favoritism. Wouldn't it have been so much easier to make the team the first time if you had made the offer before tryouts instead of after? Wouldn't an offer like that give you a huge advantage over the others on the borderline?

Let's face it, the star players don't have to worry about how to make a team. They are the best. They get chosen for their special talents. But what about those on the end of the bench? What does the coach of a basketball team or *any* team really hope to get out of the last several players on the bench? Star performances in big games? Hardly. He or she wants cooperative team players. Players who will work hard. Players who will contribute to, not drag down, team morale. Players who will be enjoyable to work with. Complainers and commentators need not apply. Over the long haul, any coach would rather have less talent on the end of the bench with good attitudes than lots of talent but poor attitudes.

In other words, the final, borderline selections are nothing *but* favoritism picks. The coach favors the players who will best fit those positions; and in supporting positions the need is for good attitude and effort, not for the best ability.

When one of those players gets a chance to get in a game, generally the coach will hope the player is satisfied enough to keep a low profile and give the ball to the others who are accustomed to winning games. Despite the story-book heroics one often dreams about—the forgotten player comes off the bench to save the day with a last-second shot—in real life, most players off the bench try to do too much and mess up the team rather than help most of the time.

Once you understand the coach's perspective when it comes to final selections, you will realize the prime importance of communication. You may call it butt-kissing if you like, but that's your problem—that's your failure to understand the importance of group dynamics to the success of a joint venture.

If you plan to go through life thinking you'll get jobs based solely on your ability and on concrete, on-paper qualifications, you will probably find you are being passed over constantly by people less qualified than you.

This is not an endorsement for compromising your standards. On the contrary, it is an endorsement for knowing precisely what your standards are, knowing what you really want, and then being willing to do whatever it takes to get that, including conveying a positive attitude to a coach or boss.

While others are mumbling about favoritism, feel free to tell them calmly, objectively, and succinctly about "the exigencies of the situation."

The exigencies of making any team begin with getting along with the person in charge, and making sure that he or she knows you are willing to do anything necessary to help get the job done as well as possible.

There are very few people in the world who are not moved
by a sincere note of thanks or a word of recognition.
Sure, your letter may get lost in bundles of others.
But that's where creativity and persistence come in.

How to Get to Know the Right People

Almost everyone is familiar with the phrase, "It's not what you know, but *who* you know."

No doubt, to a large extent it does make a difference who you know. The boss's son or daughter is more likely to take over the company than the hard-working person in the shipping department. A promotion is more likely to go to the person who plays golf with the chairman of the board.

These facts should not bother you. If you have a job that needs to be done, do you look for a friend who can do it, or do you put an ad in the paper? For most people, an ad goes in the paper only when a friend or acquaintance who can do the job can't be found. It makes sense to hire someone you know. There are fewer risks that way.

We apply that same way of thinking every day when we choose to eat at McDonald's, or stay at a Holiday Inn, or buy any brand-name product. These are places and things we "know."

With hamburgers or hotels, familiarity may not be so crucial a factor. But the more important the matter, the more important is the knowledge of what you are getting. How many people would spend fifteen thousand dollars on a type of car they had never heard of? How many would marry a person they had never seen?

An impressive resumé is fine. But nothing is more reliable than having known someone for a long time. It is impossible for a resumé to reveal what a ten-year friendship can. So face it, people will hire their friends for important positions. It is indeed who you know.

How can you make sure that you know the right people? First, you cannot always guarantee that you will. However, you can guarantee that you will know many of the "right people" if you simply do two things.

One is to impress those around you. You do not necessarily have to immediately come to the attention of the chairman of the board to get a promotion. First try impressing your boss. Make your boss look good, and when he or she gets a promotion, chances are you will move up too. Normally, the higher people move up a ladder, the more responsibility they have, and the more they need good, reliable help. If you have helped a person look good on one level, he or she is likely to assume you will be able to help at the next.

In many cases, it is not even necessary that your boss be promoted to help you. I remember being very impressed by an Aruban tennis player. He was not only very talented, but I had seen him often patiently giving tennis lessons, hour after hour, under a hot tropical sun. When he later expressed an interest in getting training or certification in the United States so that he could make a living as a tennis pro, I told him I would see what I could do.

Having no experience in tennis and knowing no one in the sport, I picked up a copy of *Tennis* magazine and looked through the advertisements. I picked the most famous tennis camp of all, which so many current stars once attended, the Nick Bolleteri Tennis School in Florida. I wrote Nick a letter, explaining how I had gotten to know Eddie Ras in Aruba, how he had impressed me with his personality and his willingness to work long and hard in the hot sun. Without any more information than that, Nick hired Ras to work for him—at a very generous salary—and certified him to teach as a tennis pro when he returned to Aruba.

Ras, who still teaches tennis, got a break by knowing someone who wasn't "someone" in particular, but who was merely impressed enough to write an enthusiastic letter on his behalf.

The written word has power. It isn't always immediate power, but your dreams or hopes are seldom fulfilled immediately. Success is usually a slow, gradual process, not something you achieve overnight. Had Eddie Ras asked me to write a letter for him the day I arrived in Aruba, I may have refused, or I may have written an unenthusiastic recommendation. A letter works best when it doesn't have to be begged for—when your work has impressed someone sufficiently that it is a joy for the writer to write it. That way, it is likely to be seen on the other end for what it is—a sincere sharing of information.

This brings us to step two in getting to know the right people: Write letters.

Naturally, the letters you write on your own behalf are not as forceful as those written for you. But there is no reason you cannot try to change that to make the power of the written word work for you.

First, make a list of the people you would like to know. Get their addresses. Learn about them. What are they interested in? What are they involved in? What are they accomplishing?

There are very few people in the world—regardless of how important they are—who are not moved by a sincere note of appreciation or thanks, or by a word of recognition. The greatest athletes not only appreciate the applause of fans, they absolutely depend on it. The same goes for movie stars. Even presidents need the support of people. They need—and often refer to—the positive letters they have received. Sure, your letter may get lost in bundles of others. But that's where creativity and persistence come in. Can you make your letter stand out from the others?

Your letters are better directed to those who are not right at the top. Obviously, a star past his or her prime or a struggling rookie who hasn't made it yet would probably appreciate a letter more than someone who just won an Academy Award. Perhaps you need to alter what you are sending. One fan letter among thousands will undoubtedly get lost in the shuffle. But what about a letter sent Federal Express, with an article enclosed that you think will particularly appeal to this person, based on something you have read or learned?

Imagine the force of letters sent over a period of time, all containing information of particular interest to the person to whom you are writing. How could they be ignored?

Consider getting an unusual kind of stationery. Design it yourself with your own personal logo, or perhaps a slogan on the top that particularly appeals to you.

So, now what? You have special stationery and you have your list. Keep in touch! Your first letter can say merely that you are writing a note just to express your appreciation for whatever it is you appreciate about that person. It doesn't have to be long. Two sentences will be fine. Your second letter might include an article—preferably about the person. A later letter might include an article about you.

It may seem like bragging to send someone an article about yourself, but it is often done; and few people take it as self-aggrandizement. Usually an article about someone is quite welcome. We all read the paper and are accustomed to reading about others. Besides, it is nice to read good news, and nice to know someone who sends good news.

Finally, what do you have to lose? Unless your letters are filled with silly things that give a negative impression, you can only help yourself by giving others an opportunity to become acquainted with you.

If you are a plumber, how can you know when someone needs a plumber? The only way is to let them know that plumbing is your trade, and then wait to see what happens. Many people will never utilize your services, but some will. That's why you make a whole list of people you would like to know, rather than choosing just one.

Don't overdo it. Don't feel you have to bombard everyone three times a week. Just keep in touch and remain aware of what is going on around you. The effort will pay dividends if you keep to it. More than likely, you will meet some of the people to whom you are writing, if you attend the kind of functions they do and continue to make progress in your own profession; and when you meet you will probably be surprised that they remember you.

They may have nothing for you, no way in which to help you or use your talents or skills, and then again, they may.

One thing is sure. It never hurts to send off a few letters of congratulations and thanks, and an article or two about yourself, to the people who could have a profound influence on your career.

If people ain't anticipating something happening,
they're gonna mess up sure as your Granny's gonna offer
you some food when you visit her house.

SP = A + AP:
How to Perform at Your Peak
in Everything You Do

Letters in equations sometimes take some rather simple idea and give it a more scientific air. I have done that here to make sure you don't miss the importance of this crucial concept: Most people who perform extremely well (SP = Successful Performance), whether it be running a race, giving a speech, or offering a piano recital, have had the benefit of A + AP: Anticipation plus Advance Preparation.

This may sound like something you already know, but it probably has many more applications than you ever imagined. You say, "Of course the person playing the piano knew about the recital and knew what to play, and therefore had plenty of time to prepare." True. But does that make the preparation any less valuable? There is a lesson to be learned. A + AP are essential for everything you do.

Let's put it a different way.

Nearly everyone, without exception, when called upon unexpectedly to do something, does it poorly. Maybe there is someone somewhere who has pulled off some dazzling feat without having prepared for it, but it almost never happens.

If people ain't anticipating something happening, they're gonna mess up sure as your Granny's gonna offer you some food when you visit her house.

If a quarterback sees a defense he has never seen before, he'll usually make some kind of mistake—get sacked, throw an interception, or fumble. The quarterback is supposedly one of the smartest players on the team, but he will not be smart when confronting something he has never seen before.

Many of the best musicians in the world, if asked to play a piece they never saw before, would simply refuse. They just wouldn't play it. They'd say they wanted to take it home to practice. They realize that their presentation would be much below par without time to prepare.

The examples are endless. If you are absent for a week and find that there's a test when you return, you will probably flunk it.

If you drive on a slippery street and you are not prepared for sliding, chances are that you will slam on your brakes precisely when the wheels should be turning. Practice in slippery conditions makes this obvious, but meet it for the first time and you will mess up.

Walk up to a person and ask for a date with no idea what to say, and chances are you will say things that later you will wish you hadn't.

The unexpected foils us all. It is our task in life to anticipate the things that are likely to happen to us, and to prepare ourselves for them.

So you are about to be interviewed for a job or a college application? Don't go in hoping they ask you some questions you can answer. Go with a group of prepared answers that you know you want the listener to hear. Then use those answers. Attach them to some question, even if you have to introduce a whole new subject by saying something like, "That really is not the crucial question here. The question is. . . ." and then answer it.

You will be evaluated by what you say more than by how well you answer the specific questions. The questions are merely devices to bring out your thoughts. In fact, they may not even matter to the questioner. The important thing is how you conduct yourself. Knowing that, you are stupid to wait around for the questions. Your task is to decide in advance what you want the interviewer to hear from you, and say those things.

The same applies to making an impression on a date. Rather than waiting to see what happens, why not take control? If you are uncomfortable when you go to dances, don't go to dances. You decide the circumstances in which you are at your best, and invite your date into those circumstances. If you've got a huge, impressive house with stables and servants, take your date home! If you live in a little shack, take him or her out!

It seems so simple in extreme cases like this, but when things get a bit more complex, people forget entirely to put their best foot forward. If you are a science whiz, show your date your home lab; your experiments will surprise and delight him or her. Let your date take part and enjoy it. He or she will have successfully entered (with your help) a whole new world.

Great athletes often seem verbally uncoordinated after a championship, when a microphone is thrust in their faces and they are asked their opinions of the game. All the grace and skill they just demonstrated on the field is dashed in seconds as they stutter for an answer and end up with, "You know, man, it was, like, it was good, man, you know what I mean, like, it was good, you know."

All they would have had to do is anticipate that microphone and have a response prepared. Imagine yourself watching television and hearing an athlete who had prepared a response.

Let's look inside that preparation process. "Give credit to others, use some big words known to everyone but rarely used in every-day speech, introduce some ideas not at all related to sports, add one unusual insight." Hmmm. Good formula. Now for putting it together: Give credit to the coach. And a special fan. Use some big words (get out the dictionary or thesaurus) from other fields, such as the military *(strategic posture, frontal assault),* law *(preponderance of evidence),* space flight *(orbital trajectory),* foreign phrases *(sine qua non, laissez-faire),* ballet *(pirouette),* and, let's see, biology? chemistry? philosophy? politics? Let's try economics *(deficit spending, recession, depreciation).*

Find some words, and try to incorporate them into the ideas to be expressed. And when the announcer asks how you felt about the big win, you can say something like, "Coach Jones altered the trajectory of our practices during the past two weeks to give us an unassailable strategic posture. We were not susceptible to a frontal attack; and the preponderance of evidence clearly indicated we could pierce their defense. So we went into the game confident. Besides, my little brother had been studying films of our opponents, and he offered a suggestion we were able to use effectively. 'The sine qua non of beating State,' he said, or something to that effect, 'is laissez-faire. Don't hold anything back.' And we didn't."

Can you imagine an answer like that? That would have people across the nation buzzing. Naturally, it wouldn't have to be that overdone, but why not inject a few words here and there that indicate you are educated? Why not throw in a name from current events, showing that you read the paper and are aware of the world around you?

Given a few seconds to make an impression, why not make a good one, or an astonishing one? Why not do something other than stumble and stammer and come out with "you knows" and "mans"?

"We approached the game the way Gorbachev approached Perestroika. We knew it would not be easy, but we knew what was necessary, and we made those reforms in our game plan."

On a date . . .

"Excuse me, you have some very intriguing features that I've been thinking about, and I have a special plan for you. Can you make some time to talk with me sometime next week?"

Give a compliment. Arouse some curiosity.

Things like this aren't the kind of thing you are likely to say on the spur of the moment. But if you take time to think, to anticipate, and to prepare in advance, your presentation of yourself can be much smoother and more polished.

Before going on, why not think about all the things you do during the course of your life? When do you have the opportunity to present yourself? What opportunities are coming up in the near future? What advance preparations can you make, so that your "presentations" of yourself are the best possible?

Success is *not* the result of having the will to win, but of having the will to *prepare* to win. This makes sense not only in sports, but in everyday life.

Advance preparation is the key to successful performance—in everything you do.

Your individuality needs to be spelled out
in more than fads and fashions.
If everyone in your school wears jeans and you don't,
that doesn't make you an individual.
It just means you're wearing different pants.

How Not to
Squander Your Rebellious Spirit

Are you rebelling against something? There's nothing wrong with that. The world is filled with things that *need* to be rebelled against. Regardless of what is bothering you, you probably have some very legitimate gripes. So now what? What should you do?

The crucial point about rebellion—in anything—is to do it intelligently. Probably most important is to make sure you do it in a way that benefits you. Think about that carefully. Unfortunately, many people—especially young people—rebel by hurting themselves. Let me give an example or two.

You don't like the way they do things at school. The principal hands down stupid rules that you don't think are fair, so you decide to rebel. You refuse to abide by the rules, and you get kicked out of school.

Getting kicked out of a stupid school may be fine if you can move immediately into a better school. But chances are that is not the case. (If you have the opportunity to get into a better school, do it. Don't wait until one school kicks you out.) Usually, rebellion against a school is a thoughtless, impulsive, angry act. As a result, you are out, gone, losing a valuable opportunity for an education, and the school goes on standing.

What have you gained by getting kicked out? Nothing. But you've definitely *lost* something. It is very important to develop your self-control enough that you don't rebel in a way that causes *you* to lose out in the process. The school may be stupid, but you need an education to accomplish things in life. Better then to wade through the stupidity, maybe even to point it out in creative ways or to attack it, guerrilla-style, so that it gets hurt, not you.

For example, you could pass a petition around the school, asking students to sign their name to support some proclamation or statement. The statement might list all the things you are dissatisfied with, or the main things. Getting signatures on a statement like this won't change them overnight, but it will get some people squirming a bit, and maybe that's all you need. If you need more, think of something creative.

The point is that you must make sure to do things that benefit you. You should in no way do something that can hurt you. If you must do something, and you are filled with a spirit of rebellion, then search for something that will both satisfy you and help you. Getting yourself thrown out of school—or into prison—is hardly going to help you. That's why you should avoid throwing a brick through the school's biggest window. *You* get in trouble for that. You end up looking like a criminal while the school comes out looking like an innocent victim.

Instead, make sure the school looks bad. Write a page about the problems in the school, get the page copied, and secretly put it in places where you know it will be read—on teacher's desks, under the door of the faculty lounge, in the main office, on cars in the parking lot.

If you have legitimate gripes, write them down and let the world see them. Words have more power than you think.

You have more power than you think, but not if you squander it by destructive acts.

You may want to rebel against your parents' lifestyle, so you start hanging out on the street corner using drugs. What kind of rebellion is that? Where will that lead you?

How to Get Your Pride Working for You

Pride. Most people don't think of it in terms of a tool, or something that can work for them. But that's exactly what pride should be. Unfortunately for most people, their pride usually works against them.

In perhaps the most typical example, people develop pride in a kind of perverted toughness, one that says roughly, "I don't take no crap from no one." What is the result? Unnecessary fights, excessive responses. Often these lead to physical violence, jail, or death. The pattern is familiar. Someone gets insulted, pulls a knife and stabs someone else. He or she goes to reform school or prison and still, "I don't take no crap from no one." This person spits on the guards, never gets paroled for good behavior, fights with inmates, and ends up dying. It's a gruesome scenario, but one that is all too common.

Too quick to tell a teacher to go to hell, too quick to call a woman a bitch or a man a bastard, too quick to throw a punch. You know the type. Somewhere along the line, they learned to put their pride in "not takin' nothin' from no one," instead of developing a different kind of toughness—tolerance, patience, and thoughtfulness.

It isn't easy to walk away from a fight, especially from one you know you can win. It isn't easy acting respectfully to a teacher who may not deserve your respect. But it gets much easier once you place your pride in yourself as a winner, as a tough-minded person who will not be distracted from the road to your personal success.

Do you have time to interrupt your life with a three-year jail sentence? If you are proud of who you are and where you are going, you won't be drawn into a fight that would put you off your chosen path.

The proper placement of your pride reaches into many areas of everyday life. Its negative placement is not at all limited to the lives of convicts and criminals.

Consider students who sit in the back of each class, just waiting for the bell to end each period so they can get out and be with friends. Where have they placed their pride? "This course is stupid; school sucks; that teacher is boring." You've heard these things. They are not a product of the careful weighing of options and alternatives. They are the thoughtless, rebellious mutterings of kids who are ignorant of the ways of the world.

Of course, school and teachers and subjects can be boring. But are these kids doing their best to make the best of it? No way. They are putting in time, feeling a sense of one-up-manship, because they think they are above this stupid stuff.

As soon as the bell rings, do they run home to work on their chosen careers? Hardly. They hang out, they waste their time. They are on paths headed nowhere. They don't realize their errors, and their misplaced pride forces them to wear blinders, so that they don't see what they are doing.

In most cases, they become proud of the clothes they wear, or the way they wear their hair, the cars they drive, the drugs they take, or the weapons they carry. This is pride in the most superficial things of all, but they don't see it. Pride is a powerful force, and theirs is misdirected, working against them, not for them.

This is no roundabout way to get you to listen in class and care about books. Your life is up to you, regardless of what some author says. I will never meet most of the people who ever read this book. I will never know if they chose to make the most of their lives, or if they got killed in knife fights.

I will never hear about the kids who saw these words and said, "Bullshit, DeVenzio, you don't know what you're talking about." I will have to assume that they didn't read, didn't consider their alternatives, didn't think about how they were living or what choices they were making. I will think, as I always do, what a shame that they didn't see that pride must be placed where it can work for you, where it can teach you to sit in front of the class and tolerate the snide remarks of "cool" kids who call you "teacher's pet" or "brown-nose."

Many young people are going through their lives, using up their healthiest days, and no one has yet taught them to be proud of their ability to stay attentive when a class is truly boring, or to study when they don't want to, or to run on a track when they feel lazy, or to hang in there when a teacher gets angry and criticizes them.

They have learned to say, "The hell with it," and they have mistaken that for toughness, because they "don't take no crap from no one."

Many will go through their entire lives and never learn. Just make sure that doesn't happen to you. Ask yourself every day if your pride is working for you. And if it isn't, make it work for you. You can do it.

Substance Versus Style

The crucial issues involved with your rebellion and with yourself are substance and style. Is your rebellion purely stylistic—a way of acting, a way of dressing—or is it substantial? Is there something more to it?

You may think that you are rebelling against your parents or against your principal by wearing ragged clothes or black leather or gawdy colors, but if your rebellion is merely a matter of what fabrics and colors you put on your body in the morning, yours is a very shallow rebellion, and there is not much substance to the self you think you are expressing.

Your individuality needs to be spelled out in more than fads and fashions. If everyone in your school wears jeans and you don't, that doesn't make you an individual. It just means you're wearing different pants.

Don't fool yourself. What is it that expresses a person's individuality? It is what that person believes, what that person is committed to. The only way to show who you are is by what you do. Not by what you wear, but by your actions.

What do you do? If your rebellion consists of sleeping during a class, we know nothing about the class but we *do* know that you are a sleeper. You may argue that your sleeping has some greater meaning, that it is a protest gesture, but you have to remember that people—all people—express who they are by what they do.

What Is Your Substance? What Do You Do?

You are fooling yourself if you spend your time merely reacting negatively to the things around you. Instead, you ought to get into the habit of being fully a part of the things around you until you are smart enough and creative enough to rebel against those things intelligently. You need to do things for yourself, not just sleep through things you dislike.

So, what can you do? Express yourself through sports, through music, through working with your hands, through writing or poetry, through organizing people, through a money-making venture, through a movement or cause. Through something positive.

If you must sit in a boring class, make the best of it. If you can get out of it, then get out of it—and do something you consider more constructive. But teach yourself to give yourself fully to whatever you are involved in, until you are able to get yourself out of it.

Pursue something. Become an expert. Get good at something. Do something. You cannot express yourself by merely acting *against* things.

If you are satisfied that you are "different" and unique because most people's favorite color is blue and yours is chartreuse, you are a very minor person! Don't forget that you define your identity through action. Don't fool yourself. Ask yourself if your rebellious spirit is being used intelligently. Ask yourself if your individually is based on anything substantial.

Ask yourself how you are spending your time. How would your life look on film? Could we make a good, instructive movie on what you are doing with your time? Or would even you be bored with it?

Let's explore this film idea further.

Your whole life—every hiccup, every cough, every sneeze,
every frown, every smile—is on film.
When you die, you are led into a theater by an usher
who brings you a soda and a box of popcorn,
and asks if there is anything else you want.

How to Get an Objective View of Yourself: Putting Your Life on Film

Have you ever considered what a film of your life would look like? Imagine that the producers of "Sixty Minutes" decided to secretly capture your life on film.

They would record everything—how you wake up in the morning, what you eat for breakfast, how fast you eat, what you talk about, how you begin your day. In your classrooms they would have their cameras on you the whole time. What would they see? What would they hear between classes? What view would they get of your spare time? What do you do after school? How hard do you work to improve? Are you a good sport? A constant complainer? How do you relate to your classmates? What do you do on the way home? What is your dinner like? How efficiently do you spend the hours before you go to bed? Do you put off studying? Do you study at all? Do you talk on the phone? How well do you sleep?

It may help you to imagine that a show like this was being produced for a curious audience in Japan or Russia, so that a Japanese or Russian film crew was following you everywhere in order to show a curious audience back home "A Day in the Life of an American Student."

Would your life on film be instructive? Would it give those foreign viewers insight into the greatness of America, or into the decline of America? Would they be surprised at how you use your time? Would they be impressed by your diligence? Dismayed by your laziness? Would the things you do and say and think about each day be entertaining for them? Perhaps a better question is, are the things you do and say and think entertaining for *you*?

Many people would be shocked at the way most Americans waste opportunities and time, and perhaps shocked at the careless way you approach your life. A lot of people would undoubtedly be struck by how superificial many Americans' lives are. They would wonder at the things you laugh about. They would fail to understand your sense of humor. They would probably be astonished in most cases at American students' lack of knowledge of the world around them.

Would you be eager to have your life examined so that others could get an intimate view of what makes you strive, laugh, worry, and think?

A Vision of Hell

Some people think of hell as a place burning with fire. My own vision is very different. Try to imagine it. Is it hell—or heaven?

Your whole life—every hiccup, every cough, every sneeze, every frown, every smile—is on film. When you die, you are led into a theater by an usher who brings you a soda and a box of popcorn, and asks if there is anything else you need.

You say no. You are quite comfortable, surprised that death, so far, seems so easy. Comfortable chair, empty theater, you have the best seat in the house, and the movie comes on in vivid Technicolor with Dolby stereo sound. You're hoping they show an endless series of your favorite films, all the Academy Award winners since 1953. But instead, the film is of you. From birth to death, nothing left out. You brushing your teeth, arguing with your parents, going to the bathroom, dancing, laughing, kissing, studying. It's all there, playing over and over again for all eternity as you sit and watch. You don't sleep, you don't get up to stretch or get some more popcorn. This is a theater from which you can never leave. Your fate is to watch and rewatch your brief life on Earth. And then. . . .

A Voice from the Sky: One More Time

Imagine you watched that film of your life for several hundred years. So you could see your entire life over again several times. You would know it well by then. What would you want to change? What if you had it to do over?

What if the screen suddenly got dark and a voice suddenly boomed down into the theater?

"You will have one more chance, one more time, one more life on Earth, filmed once again in every detail, in Technicolor, in Dolby sound. Then you will watch again, this time for seven thousand years. Good luck."

Next thing you know you are kicking and screaming, and you have a vague awareness that you have just been born. You are starting all over. Your life is waiting before you. How will you go about it? What will you do? What things will you want on that film, knowing that you will have to watch it over and over, examining it in every detail?

Should I bring a camera to your house tomorrow?

*Many students think they must hide their poverty
from the Admissions Office so they will have a better chance
of being accepted. That is not true at all.*

How to Get Money for College

Many people don't realize how much financial aid is available for college. There are thousands of students throughout the nation, with no special athletic ability and no outstanding grades or test scores, who are going to college for free.

Many of you have already heard of Pell Grants, SEOG (Supplemental Educational Opportunity Grants), and work-study programs, so I won't make this section a long one. Let me just make it clear that lack of money need *not* be a reason to bypass college.

How do you get the money that is available? Simple. You apply to a college and, if you qualify for admission, then you check with the Financial Aid Office (every college has one) and find out what grants and programs you are eligible for.

Many students think they must hide their poverty from the Admissions Office so they will have a better chance of being accepted. That is not true at all. The admissions people have no concern whatsoever for your financial status. If you qualify, they will be happy to admit you, regardless of your financial situation. And the Financial Aid Office will be happy to lay out for you what you must do in order to get the grants and jobs and loans needed to get you through. That's their job. They will be happy to help you.

I have been surprised in recent years at how many misconceptions there are concerning money and college. Even commercials on television add to the misconceptions; they show a few kids sitting around a table talking about not having sufficient money for college—then one points out that money is available through the Army.

Money *is* available through the Army. But there are many other ways of getting it. The most simple is a letter to the Financial Aid Office that asks one question: "Can you help me find out how I can get money for a college education? I have been admitted to your school but have no money and no support from my parents."

They will find a way to do it. Kenneth A. Kohl, a recent Commissioner of Education, once said, "I am confident that any student in America can get a college education . . . no matter what his [or her] family's financial resources are." Even today this is the belief and policy of the Secretary of Education and of Congress. And I have seen it work enough to know that you *can* go to college and find the money to pay for it, if you merely make an effort to seek the funds that are available. You may not be able to go to the one and only college of your choice, but certainly you will be able to get a good education.

The crucial point is this: Don't fail to go to college because you have no money. There *is* money available for students who want it.

*Realize that introductions are almost always difficult.
Make them enjoyable by getting
into the habit of introducing yourself.*

How to Shake Hands

This probably seems like a foolish subject to include in a how-to book. But it is foolish to go through life not knowing how to shake hands. It is also foolish not to take advantage of this ability whenever possible. Handshakes, which take all of three to five seconds, can and do make a tremendous impression on people. Done improperly, they leave a very negative impression. If not done at all, they fail to leave any impression. Are you beginning to get the idea?

It is never wrong to walk up to someone, extend your hand, say "Hello," and offer your name. In fact, if you are with someone who may not be sure of your name or those of others present, you can turn an uneasy situation into a relaxed, enjoyable situation simply by taking the lead and introducing yourself. Remember, it is never wrong to introduce yourself, even if a friend suddenly apologizes for not having already completed introductions.

Realize that introductions are almost always difficult. Make them enjoyable by getting into the habit of introducing yourself.

For the actual handshake, be firm and grab the entire hand, not the edge of the person's fingers. Firm means that you should use some pressure. Nearly everyone should grip tightly, because few people are so strong that they will cause anyone discomfort; if people begin telling you that you are hurting their hands, ease up.

If you remain in doubt, practice on a friend or two, and ask them how much pressure feels good. A handshake should convey warmth, pride, and good feelings, something you cannot do by extending a limp hand that you merely invite the other person to grasp. You should grasp a hand as though you plan to hold on—and look the person in the eye the whole time you shake. People will respect you more if you look them in the eye. Who wants to meet someone who averts their eyes?

Handshakes are so important—and so effective—that we teach them and practice them at all of our Sports Foundation leadership seminars. The participants always initially think that it's crazy to practice handshakes, but soon realize that these handshakes offered to banquet speakers, celebrities, and visiting instructors never fail to impress.

The nationally acclaimed sports broadcaster, Jim Lampley, spoke at the Ambassador Athletes Convention in the summer of 1987, and after he finished, a hundred kids all walked up to the head table and stood in line to shake his hand. He looked at me and said, "You told them to do this, didn't you?" but his suspicion didn't matter. He was touched anyway. He thoroughly enjoyed shaking one hundred hands, looking in the eyes of one hundred people who knew how to shake hands and were not embarrassed by introductions.

Is that overdoing it? In my opinion, failing to take advantage of an opportunity like that would have been *under*doing it. After all, shaking hands is easy. Most of you already know how to shake hands and look someone in the eye at the same time. But how often do you do it?

If it sounds funny to you to walk up to your teacher or coach each day and offer your hand and a few words, then *do it for fun!* But do it. Start shaking some hands *every* day. The effort will pay off in ways you may never suspect. What do you have to lose?

Jim Conley's suggestion is to begin announcing your intentions
before *you make a purchase. As soon as you begin thinking*
about a need or desire, make sure your friends
and associates hear about it.

How to Get Things You Need—Free

Jim Conley is responsible for this nugget of wisdom. He was a great college football player, captain of Michigan's Rose Bowl champions back in 1963. Conley is wealthy now, but he doesn't get his name in many books. Putting his name here may help me sell some copies. You never know. And that's the lesson that Conley imparted many years ago—and I have been surprised at how often it works:

Let people know your needs.

It sounds too simple at first, but think about it. Suppose I have an old desk I don't use. It's too good to throw away, but not really good enough to bother trying to sell through an ad in the paper. I would like to get rid of it, but I won't just toss it on the trash heap. So I keep it.

Most people have dozens of things like that—things they would be glad to give away, but they don't know anyone who needs them.

Suppose you are reading this right now thinking, "I have been needing a desk."

Why have I never given mine to you? Only one reason. I never knew you were looking for one!

Conley presented this idea long ago via a question: "Have you ever noticed how often you buy something, and you tell someone about it, and they say: 'Oh, I wish you would have told me. I have an extra one I never use. I would have given it to you, if I had only known"?"

If they had only known.

You hear that a lot because you have a tendency to share with people what you have purchased. "What did you do today?" "I went to the store. I had to buy some garden tools." Or, "I bought a new car." Or, "I bought some clothes."

Conley's suggestion, therefore, is to begin announcing your intentions *before* you make a purchase. As soon as you begin thinking about a need or desire, make sure your friends and associates hear about it. As Conley put it, "I'm thinking of getting myself some new snow tires."

Lo and behold, someone in the room had a set of snow tires that fit a car she had since traded in, but they did not fit her new car. "Hey, what size does your car take?" she asked. "I think I have some you can have."

Obviously, this is no foolproof method to satisfy your every need, but it often works.

School groups, church groups, and volunteer associations, in fact, have recognized this fact sufficiently that they often publish what they call "wish lists." On these wish lists, they will put everything from computers to pickup trucks—and often they get their wishes. A car dealer just got a trade-in, or someone has decided to get a new truck. Or a business has decided to upgrade the computers, so suddenly an old one becomes available that works just fine; the charity gets a computer and the business gets a tax write-off.

You cannot get everything you ever need using this method, but one thing is certain. You will never—or hardly ever—get something from someone who does not know you need it. People usually don't offer their old desks, or computers, or pickup trucks.

If you are the kind of person who is used to helping others, others will actually be happy to know your needs and to have the opportunity to help you sometime.

Obviously, you could overdo this idea. You could drive people crazy telling them of your needs. "Hey, you wouldn't happen to have a shiny old convertible with a nice sound system in it, would you?"

But if you use a little bit of discretion and don't overdo it, making people aware of your needs—while trying to fulfill others' needs—

makes a lot of sense. By the way, Conley, I need a nice desktop publishing system, you know, a MacIntosh Computer (Apple 2E, I think they call it) with a laser printer!

Do the things you like least first.
When you have energy,
it is easier to get an unpleasant thing done.
When you are tired, it is nearly impossible.
Whether it's yard work or studying,
get the crap over with soon.
Save the best till last.

How to Schedule Your Time for Success— And for Peace of Mind

Anyone who has several things to do at once—and every student does—can benefit from good scheduling. It may seem like an attractive concept to be free to do whatever is most important at the time, but in practice the way to obtain the most spare time possible is through intelligent scheduling.

The main points of good scheduling are simple. First, plan tomorrow tonight or, if you are a person who enjoys getting up in the morning, you may want to plan the rest of the day the first thing after waking up.

Second, write down everything that needs to be done, and then number them in the order you want to do them. Beside your "Things to Do" list you may want to draft a tentative schedule for next week as well.

Third, do the things you like least first. When you have energy, *it is easier to get an unpleasant thing done.* When you are tired, it is nearly impossible. Whether it's yard work or studying, get the crap over with soon. Save the best till last.

Those are the key ingredients for intelligent scheduling. Now, there is just one more factor to consider.

Scheduling for Peace of Mind

The most important aspect of scheduling is to know yourself, know what you are capable of, and don't schedule the impossible.

Say, for example, that you need to study four subjects for the next day, and you know you will be getting home at eight o'clock that night. You may decide that you need to put in an hour on each subject. That means, assuming you get home at eight and get immediately into studying—and take no breaks at all—that you will be studying until midnight.

Can you handle that? If so, fine. Schedule it. But if you know from past experience that you cannot handle that much, then don't schedule that much.

Why go to bed that night feeling like a failure who couldn't stick to a plan? It would be better to study the most important thing for the first hour, take a ten-minute break, study the second subject for forty-five minutes, then spend twenty minutes on each of the last two subjects with a ten-minute break in between. That way, you have some breaks, and you are finished by eleven o'clock even if you get started a bit later than anticipated.

What's so good about this method of scheduling? At eleven o'clock you feel like a success. You made a realistic schedule, got a lot done, and feel good about yourself. If you still have energy left, then you can use it. You will feel as though you are breaking world records, studying overtime. Perhaps you will go on until one or two o'clock, but it will be with a sense of momentum and success, not with a feeling of drudgery.

Only you know what you can accomplish and how much work you can get out of yourself. By scheduling yourself a workload that's just below your limit, you can give yourself a good feeling and often inspire yourself to accomplish much more. But by over-scheduling, you unnecessarily set yourself up for failure, and as a consequence can actually work at less than your best level.

When you are just "putting in time," you get a lot less out of your efforts than when you feel inspired. Naturally, you already know that. So schedule accordingly, and you will live a more inspired life.

Make a sudden, spasmodic movement
and let out a scream, just as you start to lie down.
If you are with anything but a grizzly bear,
you should get the time you need.
Then maybe you can talk about it at a less intense moment.

How to Turn Down
Requests and Say No

"Just say no." You have all heard that. It is good advice—at times. But, in other cases, you often feel as though you need more ammunition. For example, perhaps you have already made a firm decision to remain drug-free; therefore, someone's urgings are easily rejected. A simple no in that case is easy.

But saying no is more difficult when you feel ambiguous yourself, or when the request comes from a friend, or when the issue may not be as clear-cut as refusing to use drugs.

What if the issue is sex, letting a friend copy your homework, or when a classmate talks to you when the teacher has asked for your quiet attention? There are some very fine lines to be dealt with, situations that are not a matter of a simple yes or no. In these cases, it will be helpful to have some strategies, a procedure, some methods and ways of thinking and acting that enable you to stay in control of situations as they arise. When something comes up, you want to be able to act aggressively, to be decisive rather than feeling like a victim.

An overall strategy requires awareness of a few basic elements of offense that you can employ. These include lying (!), "raising the ante," and "selling the seller."

Lying for the Sake of Honesty!

Few books advise people to lie for any reason. We have all heard the words, "Honesty is the best policy." I agree with those words, and I think that lying can sometimes be used to promote honesty. In other words, don't confuse these two concepts. Honesty is a broad concept involving integrity and character. Lying, on the other hand, may have nothing at all to do with character. It is simply *saying* something that is not true.

My contention is that saying something that is not true may be a perfectly logical—and honest—way of dealing with certain situations. Let me give some examples. The most obvious may be in wartime. A soldier gets captured and questioned. "What were your battalion's orders?" "I don't know. They never told me." The soldier may know perfectly well that the orders were to cross a river, blow up the bridge, and proceed to the east, yet he may be perfectly honest—to his country, to himself, to his god—by saying his orders were to stay on one side of the river, reinforce the bridge for heavy artillery crossing later, and stay to the west. It's a lie—it's three of them. But is it wrong? Of course not.

Lying may be the right thing to do in certain situations—and in some it may be the best thing to do.

In uncomfortable sexual situations, lying may be extremely useful. You may feel some pressure to sleep with someone, and you aren't sure what to do. You like this person a lot, you just aren't sure how to handle things. You want to go a little slower. (Maybe your partner does too, thinking that that is what you want.) How do you slow things down?

Ideally, you should be able to talk to your partner about how you feel. But many people—particularly young people, who have not had much experience in sexual situations—find this difficult. In the heat of passion it is almost impossible. So if you need to buy some time, make up an excuse. Say that you are ill, that you have a stomach ache. Sharp back pain may be even more decisive. Make a sudden, spasmodic movement and let out a scream, just as you start to lie down. If you are with anything but a grizzly bear, you should get the time you need. Then maybe you can talk about it at a less intense moment.

If you wish to go on saying you feel bad, you were hoping your back wouldn't act up at that time, so what? If you need a lie to buy some time, use it—as long as you are being honest with yourself.

Need another ploy? Say you went to the doctor and got an "inconclusive test." In other words, you won't know till Monday if you have an infection, or herpes, or AIDS. You simply are in no position to take any chances—for *your partner's* sake.

You can cry, you can be dismayed. You can "have no idea" how you could have gotten anything, but you had some pain, and you went to the doctor, and the doctor said the reading was inconclusive. Come back Monday.

That kind of excuse is convincing. It is doctor-talk. How many of us use words like "inconclusive" in our everyday lives? When you tell someone that, it's *clear* you've been to the doctor!

If it seems as though I am encouraging people to lie, that's an incorrect conclusion. I am not. But I am openly acknowledging something a lot of people will not—that falsehoods are employed a great deal in life, sometimes for the better, by good people. If you can use a falsehood, a lie, to your advantage and you know clearly what you are doing and why, then use it and relax. Good people sometimes lie.

Raise the Ante

In a typically difficult situation, a friend asks to copy your homework, "just this once."

There are times you may be able to say yes with no problem. Most students—as well as teachers—recognize the difference between cheating on a test and letting someone copy homework. After all, people often study together and discuss answers. This is not merely permissible; it is advisable and encouraged. Therefore, the whole issue of homework, collaboration, and copying becomes clouded. It takes it out of the realm of clear-cut cheating; and it also makes it more difficult to say no.

So what do you say? "For your own good, I will not let you copy my homework. You will get more out of this class if you do your own work. I would only be cheating you by letting you copy from me." These may seem like nice words coming from the President's Council on Education. But it is not that simple when the request to copy comes from a good friend who has done you some favors and saved you sometime here and there. After all, the friend is not asking for a free ride through life, but for help in this one case, to get out of a temporary bind. It's just that, for right now, to avoid a zero for that assignment, he or she needs your help. Now, will you help or not?

Wow! This is difficult. A lot would depend on just how good a friend was asking, or on the particular nature of the situation. Is it something that happens once a week to this person? Or something that happens once a year?

Can you ever justify sharing your homework with someone? Despite what the Council on Education may say—just say no?— I imagine there are times when I would *offer* my homework, without even waiting to be asked. However, most of the time, I would say, "No, do it yourself. I had to do it, I'm pressed for time too. That's what education's all about, learning to deal with these kinds of crises."

I said "most of the time." What about other times, the difficult times when it's not crystal clear? Then I just might try "raising the ante."

Raising the ante means changing the nature of the whole issue. It might also involve getting back into falsehoods. I would consider responding to this kind of situation with an ante-raising *new dilemma.*

Consider throwing the tough decision back at your friend. That is what is meant by staying on the offensive, being aggressive, or raising the ante. Tell your friend that you just don't know what to do. *You* would love to just hand your paper over, but you *just promised* your mother that you wouldn't do that. For some reason, that is *very* important to your mother. She got thrown out of school once for some such thing, and now she's paranoid. She made you promise. . . .

Do you see the sudden difference? Before it was a simple matter of a homework paper, something your friend perceived as basically unimportant, that you could easily give. But now, you have changed the nature of the issue, and your friend is asking for a whole different thing—to break a solemn promise you made to your mother about an issue that happens to be very important to her.

The unspoken issue suddenly hanging in the air is: A friend might ask a friend for a harmless homework paper, but a friend should not ask a friend to break a solemn promise. By raising the ante, raising the stakes, you are not refusing the original request. You are refusing on new, unanticipated grounds. Your friend never dreamed that he or she was asking you that, and will likely respond, "Oh I didn't realize that. I'll just get it from someone else."

If, on the other hand, the reaction is, "Oh c'mon, she'll never know," then you have a reason to pause and stare at your "friend" and be upset with that brand of friendship. "You mean you are asking me to break a solemn promise to my mother over a little thing like a homework assignment? I can't believe you would do that!"

The value of raising the ante, and putting the person making the request back on the defensive, should be obvious. It can be your broad-based strategy for dealing with all sorts of situations..

Whenever you receive a request that makes you uncomfortable, you pause, suddenly looking pained and reflective. While you are looking that way, think. Search for a logical way to raise the ante.

"C'mon, yes or no?" asks your friend. Mumble, "It's not that simple" as you remain deep in thought.

Using this technique, you can stay right on your friend's level, sympathizing fully with his or her plight, and wanting to help, yet totally refusing to help in the way you were originally asked to, because in your case a whole different issue is at stake.

Selling the Seller

Another version or strategy for raising the ante involves the concept of selling the seller. I can best illustrate this concept with a personal experience.

Some years ago, when I was traveling a lot by plane, the lobbies of airports across the country were filled with people trying to spread their religious beliefs. Their typical ploy was to walk up to you directly and give you a big smile and a cheery hello-how-are-you-today? Hardly waiting for your answer, they would tell you they had a nice free gift for you and begin pinning a flower to your jacket or lapel. Before you had gotten out more than a word or two, they had given you a smile, a flower, and the gift of friendship; and all they asked in return was a tiny donation for their cause, or that you buy one of their books, which they just happened to have with them.

They were well-trained and highly committed, and they made you instantly feel bad for turning down such a nice offer from such a nice person. To give a brusque no after getting that smile and flower was not easy—without a strategy.

Luckily, I had a strategy: a wallet-sized card bearing "six principles to live by." They were very simple, yet sincere. They were, in fact, the principles by which I did try to live, and therefore principles which I truly did believe: (1) Spend your time doing things you enjoy; (2) It is okay to do anything, as long as it does not hurt others; (3) Try to touch every person you meet in a positive way; (4) See the good side of things and remain cheerful, even in bad times; (5) Toughen up and be proud of being tough; don't allow little things to get you down; and (6) Put some time every day into some project, so that you can advance toward the achievement of a goal.

I had this card with my "Six Dynamic Principles to Live By" laminated, so it would stay sturdy and look good. Whenever one of the smiling, flower-pinning people came up to me, I would no longer be in a position of having to reject their requests. On the contrary, I met their smiles with one of my own, and immediately told them I was so glad to get to meet them. I had a card with some terrific principles to live by, and if they would let me, I would explain those principles to them and sell them the card—"a card that can literally change your whole life for the better"—for only ten dollars.

Would you be willing to spend just ten dollars to change your whole life?

Do you think I even got the question out? Sellers hate to be sold. They moved away from me as though they were fleeing tear gas. They wanted no part of a smiling face who wanted to sell *them* something. The moment I used on them the precise method they were using on everyone else, they backed off instantly. They could not deal with such a request. They would not give even half the time they had so pleasantly asked me for.

Are you beginning to see the application of this principle to your own life? Does someone want to save time by copying your homework?

Funny he should ask. You were just about to ask him to do you a big favor and cut your lawn on Saturday. You know, you hated to ask, but you have this chance to leave town, and you promised your parents you would do it, and they are going to get back on Saturday evening, and it just has to be done then, and you don't have any time at all to do it. Would he mind?

Tit for tat. Just make sure you get the better of the bargain. Whatever they want from you, and however they asked it, make sure that you ask for more and ask it in the same manner—right then. I'll give you this homework to copy to save you fifteen minutes, if you'll mow my lawn and save me two hours. Hey, you brought up the whole idea of helping out a friend, I'm merely raising the ante, raising the stakes.

It is easy to prepare "bargains" like this for the kind of friends who don't mind prevailing on your good nature over and over again. You know the kind of thing they are likely to ask you for, so just prepare your own request. Have it ready to deliver with joy. If they take you up on your offer, celebrate! If they refuse, that's their problem. You played by their rules!

Don't make it a question of "I'll do this for you if you do that for me." Just make your request as if by sudden inspiration, just as they did. They will make the connection, tit for tat, without you having to state it.

Elvis is sighted all over the country,
flying saucers are seen hovering over swamps late at night
(never over Times Square at noon),
and the "Communists" have been responsible
for every political setback since 1918.

How to Creatively Disengage

Disengage. Get away. Brush off. Disappear. Be free.

Sometimes at a party or a social function of some sort you start wondering if you are a magnet for scrap iron! Of course, you would love to attract a diamond, a star, some special people, but more often you probably find you attract some forlorn little creature who clings to you for security or popularity-by-association. How do you get free without being downright rude?

Several ploys have a chance of working. But two major methods are probably all you will ever need.

First, there is the sort-of-honest approach. "It has been nice to see you. I'll talk to you again sometime." If that works, great. Use it. And don't feel obligated to give a long explanation for why you are disengaging. Most people will accept the parting and understand. They too may want to meet others and are not there to cling to you. In many cases, you may be dreaming up all sorts of disengagement strategies—and so are they. That's why the honest approach should be tried first, or the sort-of-honest approach if it hasn't really been nice to talk. What's a little lie for the sake of preserving feelings?

"Excuse me, I promised some friends I would spend some time with them tonight. I'll see you later." Or, "Excuse me, there's a person I've been hoping to talk to, and I think she will approach if I'm alone for a few minutes."

The problem comes when your honest disengaging effort is ignored—and the scrap iron still clings. That's when you need to use the secret-plan method.

The Power of Secrets and Mystery

People have a certain respect for secrets (even if they can't keep them), and they have an almost awesome appetite for intrigue. It seems nearly everyone is willing to believe that mysteries are lurking everywhere, that motivations are hidden, that conspiracies are constantly being carried on by unseen forces.

Elvis is sighted all over the country, flying saucers are seen hovering over swamps late at night (never over Times Square at noon), and the "Communists" have been responsible for every political setback since 1918.

This may be so much craziness, but it will pay to use this information on your behalf, especially when you need to disengage from a clinger who just won't take a hint or respond to the simple statement that you need to talk to someone. ("Fine. I'll just listen in!")

In these cases, the best thing to do is take these clinging vines aside and let them in on a secret, share your confidence with them, make them part of the lurking mysteries and conspiracies in the shadows.

And do it right, so they can thoroughly enjoy the experience! For example, you might change your behavior suddenly. Look around out of the corners of your eyes, furtively. Then put your hand firmly on Mr. or Ms. Cling's arm and lean your head toward his or her ear, whispering hastily, "I need to talk with you."

Be tense. But try to act relaxed. Poorly disguise your obvious sense of urgency. Tell him or her to wait there; you'll be right back. And beg him or her not to leave that spot. "Please . . . uh, I mean, I don't want to prevail on you, but, if you can. . . ." Let your eyes dart once more. "Stay here till I get back."

Then split. Be gone for awhile. But not too long. Take a deep breath, and go tell your best friend. Get some refreshments. Then go back. "Have you seen anything?" you ask.

"Seen what?"

"Oh, you haven't then."

"Seen what?"

Whisper again. Admonish. "Not so loud. I can't talk about it now." Let your eyes dart again. "Listen, I have to talk to you about something important, but I can't do it right now. There are some things going on that I can't explain. Thanks for staying in this spot. You don't have to do that any more. For right now, just go on and enjoy the party and act as though nothing happened. I'll explain it all later. Just try to act normal, but don't pay much attention to me for the rest of the night."

Mystery. Intrigue. Conspiracy. Sharing a confidence. Being part of it all. This is everything the clinger dreamed of. You will be free for the evening—and free for life, except for an occasional "lurk" or "dart."

What will you say next time you see the clinger? Easy! That you appreciated his or her discretion, but you still can't say anything. You wish you could. You will as soon as you can!

Should you really do all that? It all depends on what kind of person you are. In my opinion, life is a lot more interesting when you play a game and use your imagination, rather than when you stand around feeling strained and uneasy in an uncomfortable social situation.

Most excuses are seen as the inept attempts that they are. But excuses or disengagments that call for secrecy, intrigue, mystery, and conspiracy work every time. Why not use it on your behalf? It's not lying, exactly. It's playing! And it's fun. These things can add suspense to mere humdrum.

If you need to, think of yourself as a short-story writer. Or the director of a television show. Imagine starting a show with a woman doing some dishes or running a vacuum cleaner for ten minutes. That would be of no interest by itself. But if you begin with a bear prowling near the house, and some suspenseful music, suddenly the cameras can show that same woman again and again, and the audience stays tuned in.

Why live in the humdrum when you can introduce a feature

that transforms the whole experience—for you and for those clinging to you?

It's a short life. You're supposed to enjoy it. Put a little imagination into it. Add some of the stuff of which spy novels are built. Why not?

The very thought of improving on the sly,
when the competition wasn't even awake yet,
propelled my efforts and gave them a vitality and
concentration they otherwise would not have had.

How—and When—to Get Ahead

Everyone seems to want to know how to get ahead. You hear that phrase often. Parents want their kids to get ahead. Kids want to get ahead. Presumably, headless people want to get a head even more!

I make a joke of it, because the whole concept of getting ahead is so nebulous and murky. What's "ahead"? Is it being the president? King? Having a good job? Having a wife or husband and seven little kids screaming at the dinner table?

In reality, getting ahead doesn't mean much. Throughout your life you will be ahead of some people and behind others. You will be good at some things, bad at others. You will never get ahead of everyone at everything, nor will you ever be behind everyone at everything.

This is obvious, but it is important to realize. All of you reading these words are "ahead" of many by virtue of the fact that you can read, and that someone cared enough about you to put this book in your hands, or you cared enough about yourself to seek it out.

So, congratulations! You opened this section to find out how to get ahead, and you have discovered that you are already ahead. Now what?

I took pains to begin this section in this manner, in order to try to help you learn to enjoy success and live with it comfortably.

Some people always have a new goal—which is terrific—and they are always intensely dissatisfied with where they are—which is not terrific.

It is good to be restless and eager to move forward, but not to the extent that you spend your life chasing rainbows, never stopping to enjoy yourself along the way.

Stop now. Enjoy yourself. You are ahead. You are at the place now that you will look back on later and say, "Those were some good times."

You are young, capable, and interested in making more of your abilities. You take that for granted, but you shouldn't. You should be happy as nine larks every day—for the opportunities that are within your grasp.

How do you get them?

When to Get Ahead

The best way I know to move yourself to further levels, to get ahead of where you are, is to use the mornings before school or work. There are two important reasons.

First, to move yourself forward you need to set aside time each day to chip away at your goal. You need to be able to make a schedule and stick to it and make sure that a daily effort is made toward the goal you are trying to attain. With all the demands on your time—and the things that will likely come up during and after school or work—it will be nearly impossible to advance steadily toward any goal during the day and evening hours. It is simply too hard to find the time you can commit daily to be sure that your program of achievement is going steadily forward.

By committing yourself to getting up in the morning before school or work, you can schedule whatever you want in that time. If you schedule an hour, then you have five hours per week—at least—to work toward your goal. At the end of the month, you'll have twenty hours. At the end of a school year, nearly two hundred hours. That is a tremendous amount of "extra" time to give to some pursuit. Spread out like that, it is likely to be effective time as well. (Much more effective than squeezing ten hours a day into twenty summer days, though your goal may require that as well.)

The second reason for using the mornings before school or work constructively is even more important—because it is psychological.

When I was in high school, I wanted with all my heart to be the best basketball player in the nation. I had made a commitment to out-practice everyone in the United States, and I was willing to do anything to achieve that goal. Knowing that I had no way of knowing how much anyone else was practicing, I simply had to practice constantly and as effectively as possible.

The mornings before school were the most satisfying time of all. It wasn't easy getting up in the dark, when the rest of the town was still sleeping, but the effort and sacrifice gave me a good feeling, and the quiet of those early hours offered a tremendous amount of hope. During those times more than any other, I developed the sense that I was moving ahead, that I was on the way to achieving my goal. Nearly everyone with whom I was competing was *sleeping* while I was advancing, getting better.

I cannot over-emphasize the importance of the feeling. The extra hours of practice I was getting were not nearly as important as the confidence I was developing. When I got chances later in state play-off games and in all-star games, I fully *expected* to do better than the others because I had put in that extra time practicing and getting better when they had been sleeping.

Perhaps you are asking how could I *know* they were sleeping. I couldn't. But I did know that very few people got up before school to work toward a goal, so surely *most* of the competitors I faced would be among the sleepers. One or two special players may have been awake getting practice too, but so be it. I never expected it would be easy to be the best. I just had to hope, if I encountered someone who had also been up early, that my time had been more eager, effort-filled, and efficient.

Maybe it had, maybe it hadn't. But when my high-school basketball career was finished and I had been named the best basketball player in Pennsylvania, and one of the top five players in the nation, I was convinced that I had gotten ahead of my competition and reached that plateau by being awake and moving forward when most of the rest of the world was asleep.

Why not give it a try? But don't be too hard on yourself at

first. Don't start out getting up two hours earlier than normal, and exhausting yourself. Try fifteen minutes or a half hour at first, and get used to the new schedule. Let the mental aspect of this new effort play in your mind. You will be moving ahead while others are sleeping—moving gradually, but certainly, forward. Get that good feeling; don't worry much about the actual work being accomplished. Don't dwell on how little time fifteen or thirty minutes is. Focus on the "extra" aspect. You are seizing time that others don't even know about.

Mornings before school—the time when acorns, unseen, stretch into giant oak trees. The time when dreams, wide awake, stretch into accomplishment. The time when you, propelled by those dreams, stretch toward greatness.

*You have to shoot the ball, make the effort, and then
let the ball bounce here and there, off the sides, off the posts,
against the top. Sometimes you can use the flippers
to keep the ball moving, but rarely can you put the ball
directly in the hole where you want it to be.*

How to Make Sure You Have Plenty of Things to Do, Places to Go, People to See

Many people are lonely. They feel as though the world is passing them by. Why don't they get any exciting opportunities? Why don't they have any enjoyable surprises? Why doesn't anyone call them?

Do you ask yourself similar questions? If you have been sitting around feeling sorry for yourself—or even if these questions just sort of nag you silently now and then—it is time for you to start rephrasing the questions. How many exciting opportunities have you offered others? How many enjoyable surprises have you given others? How many people have received calls from you?

To get the most from life, you have to give more than you get. You have to be responsible for teaching others what you want, by example. If someone once got a call from you "out of the blue," that person may return the favor years later. But few people are likely to initiate an "out of the blue" call, visit, or letter.

Few people are likely to—but *you* can. You can begin filling others' lives with some of the opportunities, surprises, and unexpected connections that you would like to have in your own life. Some of these efforts will eventually pay dividends back to you.

To have things happening in your life, you have to make sure you are "out there." People are not going to discover you if you sit alone in your bedroom. You have to be out doing things, meeting people, creating awareness of yourself over a period of time.

The Pinball Principle

Whether it is getting dates, getting a job, or getting exciting opportunities, you have to realize that life works more on the pinball principle than it does on "direction." For example, a lot of people feel lonely on Saturday night, so they consult books on how to make friends, meet people, get dates, and so on—hoping to find the solution to their problem *that night.*

As with anything else, success in dating and meeting people is built over a period of time, not during one lonely night.

When you find yourself lonely or dissatisfied one particular day or night, that is the time to begin putting your plan into effect, realizing that it will only begin to pay dividends three months later. Anyone looking for instant gratification in any sphere of life is doomed.

That's where the pinball principle comes in. Successful people understand that direct action is impossible in most endeavors. To get from one place to another, to get from where you are to where you want to be, you have to make efforts not directly related to the final result you are seeking. You have to shoot the ball, make the effort, and then let the ball bounce here and there, off the sides, off the posts, against the top. Sometimes you can use the flippers to keep the ball moving, to keep the action happening, but rarely can you put the ball directly in the hole where you want it to be. You have to shoot it, flip it, jostle things around, and keep scoring points while you wait for the result you want.

Often you have to start over, put another ball in play, and keep jostling and flipping and scoring new points. When you send a ball up toward the top right-hand corner of the machine, it isn't clear exactly how you will get the ball to fall eventually in the appropriate hole at the lower left. You have no direct control. You can influence the action here and there; and the more balls you put in play, the more points you can pile up. But very rarely does a ball just land in the perfect place, causing bells to ring and buzzers to go off and lights to light up and proclaim you the grand prize winner. In pinball you need patience, you need to make efforts that are seemingly unrelated to your goals, and you need to jostle and shake things along the way to try to influence the result on your behalf.

So would you like to get an unexpected call some day? Better make a call. Deliver a flower. Deliver homemade cookies. You don't have to be Betty Crocker to do it. It's the thought that counts. People don't expect a 250-pound football player to deliver a tiny box of cookies with a flower on it. So if you are a 250-pound football player, surprise someone. If you are a ninety-pound majorette, maybe you need to take a football with you to where the team hangs out. No one will think you would ever want to catch football. Surprise someone.

Have a party for two, a sit-down-on-the-floor affair. Or invite someone by letter to a "One Minute and Thirty-Seven Second Speech." Who can turn that down?

Are you embarrassed about where you live or by your inability to prepare the "proper" kind of party setting? Then "advertise" a special event:

"You are cordially invited to attend a hastily thrown together picnic featuring a peanut butter sandwich eating contest. Only two are in the contest, there are no prizes, but you will get plenty of recognition. Take a chance! You only live once."

Would you go? No? Well then, what would you go to? Invite someone to that. Most people will try anything once. If your invitation is turned down, so what? Your preparations didn't cost you hundreds of dollars. Put another ball in play. Put your hands on the flippers and make some things happen.

The pinball principle will work. You *will* pile up points if you continue to put balls in play and keep-a-shakin'. Failure is always a result of inactivity, of sitting on the sidelines and feeling sorry for yourself. Why can't you be like clever Johnny, or intelligent Mary, or sexy Suzy, or handsome Jim? You are wasting your time making comparisons, and you know that. During your life there will always be people with more dates, more friends, more good luck, and more money. Just as there will always be people lying paralyzed in hospitals or sitting at home in pain.

Your task is to make the most of your opportunities, and to

create your own as well. Regardless of what things appear to be like on the outside, everyone has his or her own game to play, his or her own obstacles and disappointments.

Just make sure that *your* game is seen for what it is—pinball. Put balls into play, shake and bake, and don't be devastated if occasionally things go *tilt!*

Stick a new coin in the slot and start again. Put some balls into play and pile up points. And enjoy the effort. Not every ball is going to land exactly where you aim it. But you know and understand that. You just need to be reminded sometime.

Touché?

You will be less upset
if you immediately concentrate on the words.
If you intend to report on it, to write on it,
to explain it to others—
you can actually enjoy the experience.

How to Get Through Unpleasant Situations

Your parents are arguing. Your school principal is "giving you the business." You are sitting through a boring class. You are waiting in a doctor's office.

How do you get through unpleasant situations? Hypnosis may be the answer—but we'll talk more about that later. Or the answer may be in another commonly used method that may work for you: reporting.

Reporters and writers have a big advantage over the general public in dealing with certain unpleasant situations, because they are accustomed to stepping away from the situation and viewing it objectively, gathering the facts and thinking of it in terms of a story. This habit, by itself, often defuses potentially exasperating or infuriating incidents. For example, imagine that a person is particularly rude to you. If you concentrate on nothing but rudeness, you have little choice but to be upset by it. But if you immediately concentrate on the words, on trying to recollect the exact exchange—because you intend to report on it, to write about it, to explain it to others—you can actually enjoy the experience. In fact, you may even want to encourage the rudeness so that your story is that much more substantial. Just how rude can they be? What is driving them? How long will it take them to realize what complete jerks they are? Will they ever realize it? Are they pleased to be jerks?

"Excuse me, sir (or ma'am), could you please tell me, who is your immediate superior?"

Sure, you would like their boss to know about this rudeness. Can you imagine the effect you could have if you pull out a small pad and begin taking notes? Or if you suddenly produce a tape recorder and encourage them to continue?

Few people like wars. Yet reporters purposely fly to the scene of the heaviest action. They risk their lives to see for themselves what is happening. And sometimes they are killed. But they readily choose such assignments.

Obviously, reporting does change the quality of an experience. There is no reason you cannot become a "reporter" during unpleasant situations, even if no one will ever read your story. It is comforting just to think the way a reporter thinks. And who knows? Maybe someone *will* buy your story someday. Maybe your accumulated experiences have a lot more value than you think. You won't know until you start putting them on paper. Don't worry too much about your spelling or grammar, just get those experiences on paper, in detail, and let them pile up.

Great movies and great literature are made of little more than a careful rendering of daily life. In the hands of a good artist, *every* life could be the subject of an interesting movie or book. Yours could too. Especially if you have a lot of unpleasantness to deal with.

Are you feeling inept and nervous at a dance? That's not the end of the world. All sorts of great people have begun their lives with similar unspectacular circumstances. Most people are now familiar with the fact that Einstein once flunked math, that a former Miss America was once an ugly little fat girl, that an Olympic champion was once a cripple.

Unpleasant experiences are an unevitable part of life. People argue, people get sick. People die. There are no easy answers or solutions. But you can often change the nature of your experiences—even the very unpleasant ones—by becoming a "reporter," by adopting the writer's attention to detail, the flow of events, the various aspects of the situation, the sidelights, the subtleties, the hidden motivations.

Try it. You don't have to bring along a pen and pad, or a tape recorder. But give yourself a chance to see how the writer's viewpoint can transform an experience. You may very well be elated with the result.

And don't say, "No one will want to read what I write anyway." I for one would love to get some letters from people who give this a try and find they are able to transform a negative experience.

On days when you just don't feel very energetic,
the paper chain will be a powerful force urging you
to give it a shot. It doesn't demand a world record
each time you try, but it does ask you to try.
The only way it grows is through your efforts.

How to "Paper Chain" Your Way to a Goal

A paper chain is nothing special, but it can be powerful motivation. Do you remember making paper chains in kindergarten? You get some strips of colored paper, any size, usually about an inch wide and several inches long, and you bring one end up to the other, turning the strip of paper into a ring of paper. One staple holds the ring together securely, and that ring is ready to be joined to another ring—each time you accomplish some previously planned step on your way to a goal.

Obviously, you can make step-by-step improvement without needing a paper chain to mark your accomplishments, but anything that helps—and is easy—is worth considering. Seeing a chain grow each day, or each time you make a certain effort, is powerful motivation to keep it going.

Suppose you decide you want your upper body to be stronger and to look better. All it will take is push-ups once a day. (Simply do as many as you can. When you get to that last one, when you can't do any more, keep trying for just a few seconds, then stop. That's all you need to do to improve the appearance and strength of your chest and arms. It isn't as easy as it sounds, but it certainly is doable.)

Each day, after you get down on the ground and push yourself to do as many push-ups as you can, go straight to your paper strips, get one, and add it to the chain.

Put the chain in a prominent place, in your bedroom or bathroom, where you will see it often. And watch it grow.

On days when you just don't feel very energetic, the chain will be a powerful force urging you to give it a shot. It doesn't demand a world record each time you try. But it does ask you to try. The only way it grows is through your efforts.

The effect is important and useful enough that you ought to consider having a chain going, growing, at all times. For push-ups, or studying, or jogging, you name it. You decide.

Perhaps you could even play a chain game. Have a black chain and a red chain, battling it out. Are you going to read for an hour a day, or learn a new vocabulary word each day? That might be your black chain. Exercising or some sort of physical effort might be your red chain. Why not tape them side by side, at the ceiling beside your bed, and see which one reaches the floor first? Make it a race. Mind versus matter!

If you don't like making paper chains, you can mark Xs on calendar pages, put marbles in a jar, dimes in a bank, or lines on a chart. You can mark your efforts and progress any way you like. This will help you see tangible results and get you started. Then, once you have a program going and you have made a habit of doing the desired thing, you can stop marking progress on that, and begin on something new.

Try it. Chances are you will like charting your progress and you'll be a better person for it.

When successful corporations want to try out a new plan,
a new product, or a new program,
they test-market it.

Self-Help, Corporate Style

No one who makes efforts to improve should have a negative self-image, regardless of whether the efforts are successful or not.

Nearly everyone fails to achieve their grand plans. Whether it be a super diet aimed at making you look like a movie star, or an exercise program that can enable you to win the Boston Marathon, you are likely to fail.

In other words, even the best people who begin grand projects are at tremendous risk of failing. As a result, there is a tendency for people to go through life seeing themselves, to varying degrees, as failures. Not only is this hard on your psyche, but it discourages the repeated efforts that are the keys to success in any venture. Fortunately, there is an easy way to step past this success-failure problem.

The Test-Marketing Solution

The solution to this never-ending drama of goal-setting, striving, and failing lies in a common corporate strategy called test-marketing.

When successful corporations want to try out a new plan, a new product, or a new program, they test-market it.

They have the best minds of the corporation get together and come up with new slogans, new wrappings, and new advertisements. They sit around tables and argue, brainstorm, and often hire outside consultants to check on their plans.

Once they feel certain they have everything in place and will be successful, do they jump in and do it? *You* probably would— with a lot less thinking and planning and preparation. But *they* don't. They test-market. They try the plan out. They see how it works on a small scale. Then they decide how to proceed from there.

By this method, they rarely fail. The stockholders have come to accept as natural the idea that each year the balance sheet will show test-marketing expenses.

Test-marketing is a way of learning and experimenting, and it is a necessary way of doing business.

Do you realize that corporate chairmen are rarely, if ever, removed from their positions (or even criticized), for market tests that prove to be negative? On the contrary, plans are put together, they are tested, and when they don't work, the leaders often get *kudos* for the failure!

Approval for failure? Yes. Their caution is praised. They saved the corporation millions of dollars by *not* trying an unsuccessful plan on a national scale!

Why not learn from this procedure and use it yourself? Why not consider any plan of yours as a test-market? Try something out. See how it goes.

What about that diet that you berated yourself for going off of? Was it really a failure? Why think of it that way? Why not think of it as a test-market? Was it feasible for you to live the rest of your life on wheat germ, celery, and a protein drink? No. Thank God you went off! You couldn't do it. You didn't do it. But you didn't fail—you tried out a plan, you did a test-market, and the *plan* failed. Not you. The plan wasn't as good as it seemed to be during the planning stages. When push came to shove during the implementation process, your brain took over and said, "You fool— who wants to live on wheat germ, celery, and a protein drink?"

So you didn't follow your diet plan. Are you devastated by the failure? Hardly. You are wiser now. You did a test-market, and you learned some things. You are now in the position to make some adjustments to the plan in light of the newly gained information.

A workable diet must be more in tune with "the public taste." Perhaps it has to include some occasional forays into hot fudge sundaes or double cheese pizzas.

Always Planning, Never Failing, Staying High on You and on Life!

The point of course is that you come to see yourself not as a perennial failure, but as an indefatigable tester-of-markets—always learning, always encouraged to try again, and always increasing your personal intelligence. You are always on the verge of just the right product mix, the perfect solution to your problem—because you are always shifting the focus, altering the variables, and dealing with the problems from the most positive perspective. You are always planning, refining the formula—never failing, staying "high."

There is nothing wrong with your fear,
and there is no reason to be embarrassed by it.
But if you are determined to overcome it,
to walk out to the edge
of the diving platform and leap. . . .

How to Use Ancient Wisdom
in Your Behalf

I tried to fool you on this one. I decided "ancient wisdom" would pull you in better than "rituals." But this chapter is on rituals, and rituals are something that have been recognized since ancient times as having powerful potential for molding behavior and belief.

Religions, of course, are most often associated with rituals. Whether you believe in a certain religion or not, you cannot fail to notice that their rituals are effective. They keep people's interest over hundreds, even thousands, of years. They have value. They work.

Why not use rituals in your behalf? You can create your own and make them work for you.

The dictionary defines rituals, in case you were wondering, as a "practice or behavior repeated in a prescribed manner."

The value of creating rituals for yourself lies in their ability to lock you into a behavior pattern that you want for yourself. Let me give some examples.

Suppose you want to dive off a ten-meter board, and you are afraid. Fine. Admit it. There's nothing wrong with being afraid of diving off a high place. If people were not afraid of such things, our streets would be littered with the bodies of would-be supermen who tried flying off buildings.

In any case, there is nothing wrong with your fear, and there is no reason to be embarrassed by it. But if you are determined to overcome it, to walk out to the edge of the diving platform and leap, then you may find that employing a ritual will make it much easier. Here's how you might do it.

The Easy Progression

In creating a ritual to enable you to do something difficult, you merely string together a series of steps or actions. Once you put that series or progression in place, merely concentrate on it, and don't give your mind any time or opportunity to dwell on or even consider your fear.

If I had to dive off a high platform—I'm no Greg Louganis—I would first practice in my bedroom and build a progression like this: touch my toes, stretch my back, raise my arms, lower them, step forward three determined steps, carefully place my toes precisely together touching some imaginary line (the edge of the platform), then flash a quick mental image of myself diving into the water (as though I were watching it from far away), then leap.

Step by step. I would repeat the steps over and over until I knew them well. By following the step-by-step progression, I would hope to crowd out any thoughts I had of being afraid. When the actual time came for diving, I would try to repeat those steps exactly as I had in the bedroom, so I would feel the comfort and security of doing the familiar, right there up on the high platform.

I may not get a 9.9, but my ritual would get me off the platform.

Getting Up in the Morning

Suppose you are one of those people who has great difficulty getting up in the morning, because you have spent years dwelling on how tired you are or how miserable you are when you wake up. You could benefit significantly from a ritual like this:

When the alarm goes off, touch your head with both hands, touch your toes, grab your feet, release, turn the pillow over, roll over, raise your legs, recite two lines of poetry, imagine waking up in a foxhole with enemy gunfire all around you piercing through the night, recall what you did yesterday at 7:07 P.M., anticipate what you will do today at 3:44 P.M., grab one knee, put it on the floor, take three steps on the way to the bathroom and then curtsy or bow dramatically, as though thousands are cheering your awakening; doff your cap, shrug your shoulders, and toss your head arrogantly.

Then brush your teeth.

Naturally, you may not need all those steps. (Or you may need more.) The important thing is to get a progression, and follow it, keep your mind on it, and live it. If you are bowing to thousands of cheering fans, then live that, imagine them, laugh at the absurdity of the situation—and enjoy it.

A Study Ritual

Suppose you have difficulty doing your homework. It would be best to develop a ritual that would begin the moment you got home from school. Let's say you want to be able to begin studying each night at eight o'clock, but you find you put it off to watch one more television program, and sometimes one more and one more.

Try this. Make the commercial between the 7:30 program and the 8:00 program your "alarm" or "starting gun." The program ends, a commercial comes on. You suddenly grab both ears, swivel around, make a face, squint, and push your head to one side. Go to the door and look out, as though you have heard the strangest noise. Walk to your refrigerator and give it a pat on the back. Say, "You don't get enough credit, Old Boy. You keep everything cold around here, you light up every time we open you, but still, you are taken for granted. I want you to know *I* don't forget you. I'd talk to you longer but I'm going to study!" Make an abrupt about-face, soldier-like, march to your books, put them on a platter (covered with silk if you like), and take them like a waiter to your study table or desk. Open the top book immediately and begin—pen in hand, pad at your side—taking notes, or making a mural.

Do you need all that? Of course not. But if it adds to your fun, why not? If your mother or brother thinks you are crazy, so what? Perhaps you should include them in your ritual. You simply cannot begin until you touch your brother's nose—assuming he is there!

The important thing is to establish a progression, a series of steps that appeal to you. Not a series of things that you will want to avoid as much as studying!

Usually, studying isn't that bad once you are absorbed in it. The hard part is stopping what you're doing—talking with friends, eating, or watching television—to get to work. A ritual can make that easy, even automatic. When the clock strikes eight, you can go into your act.

By doing this, you never have to make a decision to leap off a high dive, or to begin to study for three hours, or to get up out of your bed when you're tired. Your decision is merely to take the first easy step: touching your head, or grabbing your ears, or some tiny thing like that. The rest just follows in line, one action after another until you are doing the thing you had sought to avoid.

*In this experiment, the skilled race-car driver drove
a high-powered vehicle that could accelerate quickly
and stop quickly. The police gave him permission
to run red lights, exceed the speed limit, switch lanes
back and forth, pass in no-passing zones—anything,
as long as he didn't endanger any lives in the process.*

How to Drive Intelligently

Good driving, in my opinion, has little to do with the techniques
you learn in driver-education classes. Nearly everyone learns the
proper techniques easily. The problem is that people take their tem-
peraments to the streets—and their frustrations, their anger, their
impatience. Consequently, the roads are often filled with maniacs
who seem more bent on killing one another or on making narrow
escapes than on quietly moving along toward their destination.

No doubt another problem is that going fast is fun—whether
it be in a boat, on a bike, or in a car. So thousands of people
are on the highways trying to fulfill their dreams of becoming Mario
Andretti.

What can be done about others? Nothing, of course. But something can be done about *you.* Many more people get in accidents
because of their own errors than those of others. So what can you
do about your own? Several things.

First, you ought to remind yourself every time you get in your
car that your dream of being a race-car driver cannot be fulfilled
in a passenger car on a normal highway. You have to agree to give
up cheap thrills—like whizzing by some old man in a 1958 Edsel—

and demand that your good feelings come from something more substantial than winning undeclared wars or races on the highways simply because you are willing to exceed the speed limit, or because you happen to have a faster car than some old school teacher who is just using hers to get to the grocery store and back.

It is also intelligent to remind yourself, each time you get into a car, that something like fifty thousand people are killed each year on the highway. That's a lot of people. Some of your attention should be focused on making an effort *not* to be one of them. Some people call that "defensive driving"; others call it "driving to stay alive."

A Special Rush-Hour Experiment

Finally, I think the factor most influential in slowing down my driving was an experiment conducted in a major city some years ago. The experiment involved a famous race-car driver, several citizens, and the city police and highway patrol.

The experiment was for the purpose of discovering how much time a driver could save by speeding and taking risks. The experimenters realized that many accidents are caused because people are in a hurry to get somewhere; they want to save time.

In the experiment, the skilled, experienced race-car driver drove a high-powered vehicle that could accelerate quickly and stop quickly. The police gave him permission to run red lights, exceed the speed limit, switch lanes back and forth, pass in no-passing zones—anything he could do to save time, as long as he didn't endanger any lives in the process.

The race was on. The race-car driver took off from one side of the city, at the same time as several citizens driving normal cars, breaking no laws, just staying in their lanes and following the traffic. All of the cars were trying to get through rush-hour traffic, across the city, to a destination about ten or twelve miles away.

With tires smoking, the racer took off and left the citizens behind, came up to the first red light, quickly looked both ways, had time to dart through and was on his merry way, zigging and zagging through the streets to victory!

What do you think happened? Of course the racer arrived at

the finish line first. He had run seven or eight red lights, drifted through a couple of stop signs, passed in some no-passing zones, and even drove onto a sidewalk to pass a couple of cars.

The amazing thing is that the next driver to reach the destination, who had not exceeded the speed limit and who had not hurried, had broken no rules, and had driven on no sidewalks, arrived at the finish line ten miles away only three minutes later!

Three minutes! The experienced racer, driving the best car on the road, with permission to break all the rules, was only able to save three minutes. And all of the drivers in the experiment reached the destination within five minutes of the racer. The obvious point is that you simply cannot save much time on a drive across a city, regardless of what you do.

So what is so crucial about five minutes? The next time you find yourself racing through the streets because you are "in a hurry," you ought to ask yourself if your risk-taking is really intelligent, considering that (1) you are increasing your chances of becoming one of the fifty thousand dead, (2) you are increasing your chances of killing someone else, and (3) you are *not* going to save much time at all.

"It's the Journey, Not the Destination"

You have undoubtedly seen the phrase above, in some form or other. It makes a lot of sense—that you have to enjoy the journey and not simply look upon it as wasted time until you get to your destination. What is the destination of life itself? Death. Why rush through your life just to die? You ought to enjoy your life, not rush through it, just as you ought to enjoy driving—and breathing and seeing and listening to music—on your way to wherever you are going.

I think it makes sense to remind yourself often that you are living your life *right now*. In other words, when you are standing in a line of people, or waiting in a line of traffic, you may think that all you are doing is waiting, but in reality you are living your life just as surely as you are when you are watching a movie or dancing or playing a sport or eating. It may sound crazy at first, but this is your life and your time. If you are constantly hurrying to get from one place to another, you are forgetting that the journey is as important as the destination, that an hour of life is an hour of life, regardless of what you are doing during that time.

You could scoff at this, but many other people have recognized this and have learned to enjoy every moment of their lives. It is possible to enjoy opening a car door, to pause to think how difficult that would be for a dog or a horse; it is possible to enjoy moving along the streets, tires rolling on smooth pavement, thousands of cars moving in and out, stopping, starting, all with a different destination, yet all regulated by the same lights and signs and rules. In a way, viewed from high above, the movement of traffic through a city is remarkable. You are part of some grand organism. You resemble one tiny cell in the circulatory system. But how often do you pause to reflect on that? The streets are filled with impatient jerks who drive as though they think saving a minute will save their lives—when in fact it can kill them.

How many times have you sped by someone, cut in front of a car, quickly switched lanes and abruptly come to a stop at a light, only to have the slowly moving car pull up right beside you? How does that make you feel? It should make you feel like a jerk, to be driving like a maniac and find that you saved *zero* time. That slowpoke you just swore at has pulled up right beside you!

If you truly do enjoy driving fast, then have some guts. Get involved in racing on tracks against others who are trying to beat you. Don't allow yourself cheap victories on city streets by passing old people who don't even know you are racing with them!

Wise up. Don't race through the streets or through your life. You have one short life and only a brief moment of time to enjoy it. If you find yourself always hurrying from place to place, especially on the streets, you simply have not learned to live very well yet. Why not acknowledge that, and start working to improve it? Learn to experience each moment fully, regardless of where you are, what you are doing, or where you are going. You may think you are reading a book now, or waiting in line, or just passing some time, but you're not. You are living your life.

I'm not sure if there is anyone named Jacques LeMoyne
or François LaTour, but French names are usually
rather exotic or intimidating to most people, and if you offer
just a touch of an accent when you say them,
you have suddenly increased your own stature as well.

How to Be Self-Confident

Ask a high-school student to get up and deliver an address at the United Nations on the economic implications of political upheavals in Third World countries. Chances are the student will be nervous. That same student would not, however, be quite so nervous talking about what it is like being a high-school student in America, and would be even less nervous talking to a group of four-year-olds about how to tie a shoe.

Do these examples tell you anything?

They ought to. Though people generally have varying degrees of self-confidence, increasing it involves two things: your audience and your ability.

Understand from the outset that if you must deliver a speech on world economics and you don't know a thing about it, you have every right to be nervous. It would be ridiculous *not* to be nervous. On the other hand, if you are speaking on how to tie a shoe, you would have considerable reason to have confidence. You know how to tie a shoe; you have all the information you need. You can explain it, you can answer any questions, and if necessary you can demonstrate it, over and over, presumably without fail.

Your audience and its expectations as you perceive them naturally play a role in your self-confidence. Members of the United Nations would presumably be more critical judges than a group of four-year-olds, so consequently you would be more on guard.

If you are interested in increasing your self-confidence, you should (1) increase your knowledge in the things you are not confident about, and (2) learn more about your audience. For example, if you lack confidence with the opposite sex, you need to increase your ability to talk with them. Prepare some things to say that will go over better than your normal samplings; orchestrate events like a political candidate trying to make a good impression on the public. Prepare, stick to well-rehearsed ideas, and control as much as possible the settings in which you encounter others so that there are few opportunities to be surprised. You could plan, for example, to do something you are good at, so that your date is the unskilled one, not you. In this way, you will find yourself in the role of the explainer, the teacher, and not the inept bumbler you may sometimes feel like!

Know your audience. If you are trying to develop more confidence with the members of the UN—or with the opposite sex—you need to know more about them. What do they think? What are they like? What impresses them? Once you know those answers, it will be much easier to produce results that will gain approval for you—and add to your self-confidence.

Do not make the mistake of thinking that self-confidence can be gained through tricks or gimmicks. Sure, you can take a deep breath, or "think positively," but the surest way to self-confidence is to be better at what your target group wants.

Your nervousness about delivering a speech at the UN comes from not knowing much about economics or about the UN. However, if someone handed you a very well-written, compellingly logical speech, and if the members of the UN began applauding wildly at every pause, your self-confidence would obviously soar. In just minutes, you would be as confident as when speaking on shoe-tying to preschoolers—if not more so.

Lack of self-confidence, then, is a product of inability, ignorance, and uncertainty. If you want to gain self-confidence, increase your ability and learn more about your audience. Your uncertainty, or most of it, will leave you, as a result of those gains.

Walking into a Roomful of Strangers

Many people have told me they feel particularly uncomfortable walking into a roomful of strangers. "If only I had the self-confidence to do that," one young girl said, "I would feel so much more at ease in new situations or going to places where I don't know anyone."

So, if you happen to share her uneasiness, here are a couple of hints, relying on the basic formula: increase your ability and know your audience.

How do you increase your ability to walk into a room? Think of the people who seem so well adjusted. They walk in purposefully, looking around for people they know, expecting to find familiar faces and hands to shake. Why can't you do the same? What is stopping you from walking in, smiling, approaching someone, and saying, "Hello, I've been looking forward to meeting you. Aren't you Jacques LeMoyne?"

Of course he is not Jacques LeMoyne! But so what? You walked in purposefully, you put on your best smile, you offered a firm handshake, and you were so pleased to meet him. You walked into that roomful of strangers with the best of 'em!

Oh, so now you're complaining about needing self-confidence to get out of embarrassing situations! Okay. Easy enough. "Oh, you're not Jacques LeMoyne. Gee, I'm so sorry to have interrupted you."

Mistaken identities are no big thing. They have happened to presidents, kings, queens, and probably to one-eyed jacks. They are easily managed, and have often turned into friendships. So you met someone who looked interesting but who happened not to be Jacques LeMoyne. So what? Later you will be recognizable to your would-be Jacques, and it will be easy to strike up a conversation from there.

If you need a story, prepare one! Choose the name of an obscure senator from Nebraska or Wyoming. Dan Quayle would have worked just fine in 1987. "Hello, are you Senator Quayle?" No harm in being mistaken for a senator—or a pro baseball player, or an opera star.

There's nothing wrong with asking someone if he or she is someone else and then gracefully apologizing. As I have said, usually it will enable you to speak to that person more easily a bit later.

We have not yet even gotten to point two in the formula: knowing your audience. You have to remember that an audience of strangers does not care about you—a stranger—nearly as much as you think. Sure, they will turn to look if you fall, or if you come into the room holding a large snake, or wearing a hat with live birds in it. But generally, they are much more concerned about themselves, about people they know, and about people who may be scrutinizing them. To know an audience of strangers is to realize that they don't much care about you and they won't be watching you nearly as carefully as you have led yourself to believe. In a group of strangers, your opportunities are wide open.

If it helps you to walk in giving the obvious impression that you are searching for someone, then do that. Or walk purposefully through the crowd straight to the bar or the head table or the front desk—whatever—and ask directly if François LaTour is in attendance.

I'm not sure if there is anyone named Jacques LeMoyne or François LaTour, but French names are usually rather exotic or intimidating to most people, and if you offer just a touch of an accent when you say them, you have suddenly increased your own stature as well. In most cases, people will apologize for not having seen these noble Frenchmen, and they will be just as eager as you to make their acquaintance! Perhaps the two of you can become friends as you wait for them together.

Are you starting to understand something about this whole stranger and self-confidence thing? *Enjoy it.* Quit giving it so much importance. Add some joy to your life—and to the lives of those around you. Are you lying to ask for an imaginary Frenchman? Come on now! Share the story with someone. Ever heard of a *joke*? Have some fun in life. Don't spend your time tiptoeing around people who don't even know you, much less care. If a little harmless fabrication helps you to change a tentative feeling to a purposeful, sly, or mischievous one, go for it. You're welcome to it. The whole world, in fact, will be better for it. And who knows? Someday you may just meet messieurs LeMoyne and LaTour themselves. What a thrill *that* would be!

In my opinion, she had just the right mixture of flirtatiousness
and seriousness to get just about any guy interested.
She could truly have sold Porsches and smiled her way to riches.
But she turned down the opportunity to try because
she didn't know anything about cars.

How to Make Money

A friend of mine who needed a job very badly was offered an opportunity to work at a car dealership selling luxury sports cars. It was a great opportunity. She was single and attractive, and she talked easily with guys. In my opinion, she had just the right mixture of flirtatiousness and seriousness to get just about any guy interested in what she was selling. The instant I heard about it, I thought it was the perfect job for her. She would be meeting just the kind of guys she was interested in meeting, and she would have the chance to make money doing it. "Some people have all the luck," I thought, and I was happy for her. I pictured her getting commissions of thousands of dollars a week. In my mind, I already saw her behind the wheel of her own Porsche, telling this or that young millionaire how much she liked driving it.

Can you imagine my surprise, then, when she told me she had turned the job down?

Why?

Her answer made perfect sense to her, but none at all to me.

"I don't know anything about cars."

"Are you kidding?" I was flabbergasted. "Do you think the owner of the Porsche dealership would send you out on the lot to sell a car you didn't know anything about? No way. Haven't you ever heard of *job training*? That's what training is for—to make sure you know more than the customer, to make sure you have answers to all the questions that will come up so that you will have the confidence you need to sell the cars. Do you think the owner would put you out there and let you lose prospects who were about to plunk down forty or fifty thousand dollars on a car? No way. You will learn all about the features of your cars, why Porsche owners prefer them to Jaguars and Mercedes. You will learn about the details of their performance, about service, about warranties.

"All they have to do is tell you the questions asked by every customer for one week, and you will suddenly have everything you need to know just by knowing those answers. The same questions will be asked over and over again, and you will have the answers on the tip of your tongue. For you, selling Porsches will be like a country boy pickin' peas!"

It was too late. She had turned down the job. And I'm still angry— I wanted her to have a Porsche so that I could borrow it sometime!

Perhaps this is too long a story just to make one simple point, but I hope it is instructive. People constantly sell themselves short, miss out on opportunities because of their mistaken notions of what they "can" and "cannot" do. You can do all sorts of things, if you simply approach them systematically. What does it require? What steps will it take to develop that knowledge or ability? How long will it take?

My friend could truly have sold Porsches and smiled her way to riches. But she turned down the opportunity to try because she didn't know anything about cars.

In selling of all kinds, the important thing is knowing about people, being able to deal with them and understand their fears, their insecurities, and their questions; and then making them feel comfortable, reassured, and satisfied.

Selling: The Road to Riches

Make no mistake about it. Unless you are a computer whiz or a true superstar athlete, or unless you can sing and play the guitar like a whole zoo full of birds, the best way to riches for you is to learn to sell.

Anyone can make money in sales. You get a product, you learn all about it, you find out who might be able to use it, and you visit them. When they tell you that they are too busy, or that they don't need anything, you thank them, remain polite, and make an effort to reschedule an appointment.

Remember, everyone has time to learn about something that will help him or her make money or save time.

If you are selling fire extinguishers, go to a neighborhood where a big house has just burned down. If you are selling burglar alarms, you go to someone whose house has just been broken into.

The people who are selling fire extinguishers and burglar alarms— and brooms and cars and widgets—already know in most cases where to find their best potential customers. If they don't, they won't be in business long. If they do, they will be successful, and they will need help.

It's that simple. If you want to make money, sell something: Girl Scout cookies, newspapers, sandwiches in the dorm, raincoats outside stadiums. Or cars, wallpaper, refrigerators, and computers.

But you're just in high school. So what? Want a can't-miss idea? Visit every house in a decent neighborhood in December, when everyone has the holiday spirit, and sell them a certificate for a carwash you are having in March.

Is anything stopping you from hiring some fellow students to do the actual work for you? Of course not. That's business. Get your friends and make it a big social event, and they'll look forward to the next time.

Keep the phone numbers of every person you visit, so the next time you won't have to visit; a phone call will do.

You may be able to get a school club to do the work—so the money will go to "a school project." Of course, half of the money will go to you, but that's business. You found the prospects, you got the orders. You did the hard part. The profit can go to the school club, after you pay yourself for your time and effort.

Charge ten dollars a car, and pay five dollars a car to the students who do the work in March. You'll make $250 on only fifty orders, and the club will make $250 as well. How hard is it to gather fifty orders just before Christmas? Ten orders a night for five nights shouldn't be hard at all. But if you have a better idea, use it.

Just realize that the people who make big money in America, except for the obvious few who are celebrities, generally sell something. It's never too early to begin, to see ways in which you could sell something better, or easier, or make a larger profit. Most big-time, multi-millionaire salespeople started with paper routes or making cookies or washing cars or mowing lawns.

Anyone can offer to carry things or clean up or do odd jobs. Just look around you. If you keep your eyes open and see what people around you need or have to do, you will find a way to sell a product or service.

How can you make sure you are doing it as well as possible? The best way is simply to begin. If you begin mowing lawns that take all day—and get two dollars a lawn—you will probably have many eager buyers and start getting calls. It will dawn on you then that you have more yards to do than you can possibly do yourself, and you will either hire someone to do some for you—at one dollar a yard—or you will realize that you are under-charging and begin asking for ten dollars or twenty dollars a yard.

Don't be afraid to make some mistakes and learn as you go. So what if you don't begin in the most efficient way possible? There is nothing better than on-the-job training, or learning from experience.

Make one tiny effort with your next-door neighbor. If that works, why can't it work with the person across the street? Start small, get bigger. Learn. Reshape.

Don't worry that you don't know how to sell cars. Sell something. Start by selling just one of whatever product it is. Then sell another. Then sell something else. Almost all successful salespeople could sell all sorts of things well. The unsuccessful ones are always looking for "the right product" but rarely find it.

Look at yourself, and look around you. There is money to be made right where you are, if you are willing to start small and work for it.

*Getting the problem out of the
swimming-around-in-your-head stage
to the now-you-see-it-clearly-before-you stage
often solves the problem.*

How to Solve Your Particular Problems

Obviously, I have no way of knowing what your particular problems
are. But there are basic techniques for approaching them—no matter
what they are.

First, don't let your problems float vaguely around in your head
and terrorize you. To deal with a problem, it has to be clearly defined
and understood. Therefore, when you have a problem, the first thing
to do is get a pen and a piece of paper and go off by yourself and
write the problem down, in black and white.

It may help you to do it in "data dump" fashion—don't think
much, just start writing. Forget about the order, forget about what
is right or wrong, just get the elements of the problem in front of
you: who, what, why, when, how. Elaborate as much as you can.

Getting the problem out of the swimming-around-in-your-head
stage to the now-you-see-it-clearly-before-you stage often solves the
problem for you. Not that all problems go away by simply being
defined, but the solutions may become clear at that point.

For example, let's assume the problem is one involving illness—
yours or someone you love. Knowing precisely what the illness is
won't make it go away, but it will allow you to deal with it in the
best way possible.

Dealing with something in the best way possible usually brings significant satisfaction, even if no real solution exists. This comes back to the wisdom of knowing the difference between having the courage to change something and the serenity to accept it.

Most people realize that they can't solve every problem. But what really depresses them is feeling powerless to do anything, or feeling that something can be done but they don't exactly know what. Emptying your mind of the problem by putting it on paper has tremendous therapeutic value as well as practical, problem-solving value.

People who have learned to solve problems well, or at least how to respond adequately, are those who develop a kind of faith in this process. It is not a religious faith (it can be) but it is a strong faith in themselves and in this method. Lay out the problem, submit it to rigorous scrutiny or questioning. Consider all the possible alternatives. Choose one. Then go on living. The solution may not be perfect. But once you've done all you can, you will have a feeling of satisfaction. Even people who are terminally ill report some satisfaction when they reach the point where they no longer fear what might happen and begin accepting the inevitable, trying to make the most of the time they have left, and putting their affairs in order.

People get satisfaction by taking an active stance, by doing something, even if it is nothing more than arranging personal things, filing receipts or bills or addresses, and saying their goodbyes as they wait for the end of life.

When you realize this, it will help you to deal with anything that comes up in your life. Empty your mind on paper. Get it all out, then look it over, evaluate it, and decide on a course of action.

With some problems, a thorough evaluation may make it clear that you need to see a doctor or get some other kind of professional help, or perhaps that you need to confront someone—a parent, a teacher, a rival, or an enemy. Whatever the situation, you will find the answer more forthcoming once you make the effort to place the situation on paper rather than allowing it to swim around undefined in your head.

Better to see your enemy in red coats in the middle of a field in broad daylight, than to have them sniping at you unexpectedly from behind trees and buildings in the dark of night.

I am not pretending that the solution is easy.
You may require a doctor's help to put you on the right track.
But weight problems are not "terminal."
They can be solved.

How to Weigh the "Right" Amount

It can hardly be denied that nearly everyone looks better when his or her weight is right. "Right," of course, varies with your height and your bone structure. There is no perfect weight. Indeed, many young women and men seek to weigh much less than their ideal weight, because they have been influenced by fashion and the "thin is beautiful" attitude of our culture. Others overeat, and weigh much more than their ideal. What is the solution? Nearly everyone seems to be either on a diet, or overeating, or starving themselves. You may wonder if there aren't any normal people anywhere.

And there aren't—because everyone is unique. Some people don't have to worry about what they eat at all; their metabolism does everything for them. Some have to watch what they eat very carefully. Others have to make an effort to eat more than they naturally want. So don't worry about what your situation is. It is what it is, and you shouldn't think of yourself as strange. Fortunately, there are solutions to everyone's weight problems. There is abundant evidence that even very fat or very thin people can achieve and maintain an ideal weight.

I am not pretending that the solution to your particular set of circumstances is easy. You may require a doctor's help to put you on the right track. But at least you can be comforted by knowing that every sort of weight problem has been dealt with successfully. Weight problems are not "terminal." They can be solved.

Where do you begin? The best place to begin may be with one simple question to a doctor: "Doc, would you tell me objectively how much I ought to weigh?"

The reason I make such a point of this is that I have encountered quite a few people who either can't get an objective answer from their parents or friends, or don't believe what their parents or friends have told them.

You can understand this. Parents and friends are usually eager to encourage you, to lift your spirits; therefore, they may be willing to tell you that you look good when you don't. This may of course be a mixed signal. They want to communicate to you that they like you for who you are, not for how you look, so they say that you look "just fine" to them, even though objectively you may be overweight or underweight.

Doctors, on the other hand, can be expected to give you an unbiased, objective opinion in nearly all cases because they have gone to school for many years to get the opportunity to help solve people's problems; and doctors know they are not going to solve problems by temporarily pushing them under the rug. A doctor will nearly always walk you over to a chart and show you—in black and white—the range of weights that are "right" for your particular height. By putting a hand around your wrist or on your shoulder, a doctor will be able to assess your bone structure very quickly and be able to tell you whether you should be on the upper or lower end of the range for your height.

Once you see the numbers clearly in front of you, it is much easier to believe. A woman who is 5' 5" should ideally weigh between 110 and 130, perhaps a little more or less. But not 92 pounds, and not 170 pounds. A guy standing 5' 10" should ideally be between 150 and 180, maybe a bit more or less, but not 130 and not 210.

As in most things, moderation and balance make sense. Being obsessed with losing two pounds is not particularly intelligent. Do you really think that you will look that much better—or worse—based on two pounds? You won't, and any doctor could tell you so.

Eating disorders frequently cause young people, especially young women, to starve themselves and become too thin. They also cause the majority of people, old and young, to overeat and become fat. There are a variety of causes for eating disorders, from rebelling against parents to fear of failure or of success; this goes beyond the scope of my expertise. But having been acquainted with people who needed professional help for such disorders, I feel safe in offering the following advice.

You need to get an objective evaluation of yourself—and accept it. Then you need to realize that your personal happiness and fitness will likely be enhanced by getting in the weight-range acceptable for your height and body type. To do that, you need to make a commitment to regular exercise and reasonable eating habits; that is, getting nourishment from each of the major food groups, not necessarily every day, but regularly, and not overeating or starving yourself.

You may have grown up getting candy every time you did something good; therefore you may continue to associate eating with rewards, and use it to ward off depression and to feel good. On the other hand, there are many people who report that they now refuse to eat, expressing their latent resentment about having to endure the "ordeal" of the family dinner table, where their parents argued or the situation was strained for some other reason.

Again, I make no claim to being a psychiatrist. Eating disorders can be rooted in all sorts of complicated events from childhood, and I am not equipped to deal with them. I have, however, watched people surmount such difficulties with common sense, with moderation, with balance in their eating and exercising routines, and usually with support from others who have experienced similar problems.

If you are experiencing the frustration of an eating disorder, don't give up. Many people have been discouraged and depressed but have found the answer and have prevailed. You can too. If nothing has worked up to now, ask your doctor—or ask a new doctor if you have already tried yours.

If that doesn't work, write directly to the Sports Foundation, P.O. Box 25824, Charlotte, NC 28229-5824. We can at least offer a suggestion that can help you get a new start.

For specific methods to help you gain or lose weight, see the section on hypnosis in this book (pp. 271, 274–277).

An audience will give you its attention as long as you give them reason to think you have more surprises planned, more things to keep them awake and involved.

How to Make a Speech

Making a speech is just like writing a paper, except that you deliver it orally, right? No, wrong!

Yes, it's true that you should know the speech thoroughly, and that it should be interesting—just like a paper or report—if someone were to read it instead of hear it. But there's a whole other aspect to a speech that makes it a completely different matter.

First, it is necessary to begin a speech with something dramatic, outlandish, or mysterious. There are two reasons for this. One, people expect to be bored by speeches because so many of them are poorly done; therefore, they are likely to lose interest almost immediately unless you give them some reason to decide immediately that your speech will *not* be the same old thing. Two, if you do something crazy, wild, out of character, or mysterious at the beginning, it allows you to "act" a bit and control your nervousness.

It is difficult to stand before a group and look confident and poised and in control as you say, "Today, I am going to speak to you about how to give a good speech." That beginning is too dry. A beginning like that would hardly inspire an audience; you would be uncomfortable having to say that as you looked out at all the faces staring at you. (Don't worry, if you start your speech like that they'll stop staring at you—soon they'll be talking and looking out the window and throwing paper airplanes!)

Imagine the difference in the audience's attention if you began by marching stiffly to the front of the room, affixing a tiny mustache to your upper lip, and imitating Adolph Hitler urging the German soldiers of 1944 to fight on for the cause of the Fuhrer and the Fatherland!

Imitating Hitler would give you a chance to use some nervous energy, to overdo it, to grab their attention, to shake your fist at them, to wake them up and make them wonder what on earth you were doing. You could walk around pointing your finger in their faces, challenge them, accuse them of being lazy, of being boring, of being uncommitted, even ugly!

With a gimmick, you can make them think and wonder and enjoy.

Then you begin. "Communication. That's all a speech is. Getting ideas out so that people can understand and accept them—and use them for themselves.

"How did Adolph Hitler manage to reach so many people? First, he knew what he wanted to say. He knew what his audience wanted to hear. He knew they would lose interest unless he spoke forcefully and tuned in to their way of thinking. . . ."

Do you see how you could lead an audience into your major points through Hitler or whatever gimmick you devised?

Sure, to make a good speech you have to be well-prepared. You have to know what you want to say. But it is equally important that you think about the audience, their attention span, their interests. Tell them stories, give them examples, return to your gimmick.

"Imagine for a moment that Hitler had to make a speech on how to sew buttons on a shirt. Do you think he would just go through five simple steps? No way!"

So you rip open your shirt and send the buttons flying. *That* would get their attention. You planned for this. You made sure, in advance, the buttons were loosely fastened.

In brief, you plan attention-getters throughout your speech, and tie them into the subject directly. Don't rely on one crazy opening to carry you through the rest of the speech. First, decide exactly what information you must convey, then decide what crazy or outlandish or unusual or stimulating things you can do to help each of those facts get heard.

Visual aids are always good. Pull out a hot dog, or something gooey, or something that will stretch from one end of the room to the other—anything that once again forces the audience to think, "What is this? What will happen next?"

The audience will give you its attention for as long as you give them reason to think you have more surprises planned that will keep them awake and involved.

Ask them a simple question. Tell them they probably think they know the answer. Say that answer. Then contradict it. "No, you're wrong. You *do not* just insert the needle here and pull the thread through."

A speech requires give-and-take, constant interaction. Never rely on their being polite. Rather, force them to follow your lead; keep giving them new things to consider. Surprise them. Challenge them. Act for them. Show them. Let them feel things. Have some of them come up and try to do what you are explaining.

How do you get over your nervousness? By keeping the attention focused on Hitler, on torn buttons, on hot dogs, on people coming up to the front from the audience.

Don't make the mistake of thinking that a speech merely consists of reading information out loud. A good speech is a play, an act, entertainment prepared so that the actual information sneaks through and can hardly be recognized—yet can hardly be avoided.

Deciding what you want to communicate to the audience is the easy part. The fun part is thinking up an act, a visual aid, or a gimmick to help you "sell" each point. Sometimes the sale is Big Top, Circus, loud and exuberant; other times it should be whispered, secretive, a confidence not to be repeated. You look around before you offer it. Check outside the doors for snoopers. Check the closets.

Be loud, be quiet. Be forceful, be timid. Use a whole range of highs and lows. Don't be yourself! Step outside yourself. Be different. Be crazy. Be Hitler. Be a mouse sneaking past a cat.

Cut down on the amount of things you want to say, and add life and spice and drama to the things you do say. *That* is making a speech.

Maybe we all get so sick of being told to say "thank you"
for things we feel no gratitude for that we carry on
our rebellion through the years.

How to Perform Magic

The magic word. You've heard it. Your mother made you say it every time your grandma gave you a sloppy kiss, or every time some friend or relative gave you something you didn't want.

"What do you say? What do you say to Grandma? What do you say to the postman for bringing you that stack of mail?"

Thank you, thank you, thank you. You were probably reminded literally hundreds of times—which makes the modern-day magic phenomenon all the more astonishing. Despite the hundreds of thousands of reminders through the years, almost every person in the world feels under-valued, under-thanked, and under-appreciated.

Maybe we all get so sick of being told to say "thank you" for things we feel no gratitude for that we carry on our rebellion through the years. As a result, very few of us use the "magic word" enough. We could certainly get a helluva lot more mileage out of it.

Let me give you some examples. You may think that writers get hundreds of letters after they write a good book, but in reality very few celebrities—much less writers—actually ever get more letters than they have time to read. Most people, authors included, read every personal letter they receive, and are moved by those letters.

Newspaper reporters rarely get letters. When was the last time you wrote to thank a reporter or photographer for a story you enjoyed in the local paper? If you did, those people would think you were very special, so seldom does anyone ever bother to respond to them.

What about your mayor, your congressman, even the president? These people get a surprising number of complaints, but praise? Thank-you notes? Sincere expressions of gratitude? They don't come nearly as often as you would think—and they come even less to teachers, coaches, principals, police, and local officials.

Many of these people literally devote their entire lives to serving others, but they may go years in between thank-yous. What about your mail carrier, your delivery person, your classmates?

All around you there are people performing small but significant services for which they are almost never thanked. Do you want to perform some real magic? You will stand out from thousands of others if you comment on and thank the people around you who are doing their jobs competently or who are making your life easier through their efforts and services.

When was the last time you thanked your parents or the guardians who raised you? When was the last time you put those feelings in writing so they could read them over and over—to cherish them or to show a friend?

There's a lot of magic out there just waiting to happen. Most of the time you can take a giant step forward in people's minds with tiny actions and acknowledgements that take you from five seconds to five minutes to perform. When you begin to really think about the ground you can cover in so short a time, it becomes foolish *not* to spread thank-yous around. In fact, even if you're just a selfish, self-centered bum, it would be wise to thank people just for the incredible return you could get on your "investment." Certainly there are worse ways to be a self-centered bum. Give it a try!

*One moment you don't even care whether or not
you attend some event, but once you decide to attend it,
you may race to it, swear at obstacles, or even get into
fights trying to get there in time.*

Understanding the
Fabricated Importance Principle

You are on a highway waiting to make a certain exit, but accidentally
you go by it, and suddenly you are upset, angry, and willing to risk
your life and many others', to make a U-turn and get back to where
you wanted to be.

Why?

Moments before missing the turn you were fine. You might not
have even been in a hurry. Any of several routes was possible, but
you chose one, then let it become crucial to you.

This is what I call the principle of fabricated importance. One
moment you don't even care whether or not you attend some event,
but once you decide to attend it, you may race to it, swear at obstacles,
or even get into fights trying to get there in time.

In a way it is understandable, but in another way it is downright stupid. Consider a movie. You don't care if you go or not.
But if you decide to, you would like to catch the beginning. Me
too. But is that a reason to get yourself all excited and upset in
case you encounter some delays on your way?

It is admirable to be able to say, "Once I make up my mind,
I'm like a pit bull. I go after it." That sounds good—and it is, if
you're talking about a personal commitment, an offer to a friend,

a business investment. But no one should let this way of thinking extend to everything.

It is dumb to become angry and upset over an arbitrary decision to have fun. "Wanna go to a movie?" "I don't care, what do you want to do?" Next thing you know there's a huge argument over what movie to go to!

Don't let that happen to you. Learn to distinguish between things that are truly important to you, and things that have only fabricated importance. If more people stayed aware of the fabricated importance principle, there would probably be a lot fewer fights and arguments.

4

Getting Along With the Opposite Sex

*If you ask someone for a date, and you get anything less
than a flattered thank you—regardless of whether
it is accompanied by a yes or a no—
then you are dealing with a jerk.
And you should be happy to have learned that
so early in your acquaintanceship.*

How to Get Along With the Opposite Sex

Let's be clear on this one from the start: No one has all the necessary answers in this "game"—maybe not even half.

Guys have probably heard the joke: "Women. Can't live with 'em; can't shoot 'em."

But, seriously, I don't want to take sides here. Nor do I want to be presumptuous, as though I could tell anyone how to solve age-old man-woman problems. In fact, when I sat down to write this section, the first image that came to my mind was that of several women I once had relationships with standing together at a cocktail party, all laughing and shaking their heads.

"Can you believe it? *Him?* Writing a book about how to get along with the opposite sex? He doesn't know the first thing about it. I hope no one ever takes his advice."

That's why I am treading carefully. The title of this section might better read "Things I Wish Someone Had Told Me Before I Made Dozens of Mistakes on My Own."

I admit that I still don't have all the answers, and that I still have my share of problems in intimate relationships, but there are a lot of things I have learned over the years that I am at least glad

I know now. They now save me a lot of headaches and heartaches, even if they don't guarantee eternal bliss.

Sincere is Never Wrong

A fundamental piece of advice is: Don't worry about being laughed at or about "doing something wrong" socially. Some people are so nervous about dropping a fork or spilling a drink that they mar their dates' joy entirely.

I remember being afraid to dance because I didn't know how. What if I step on her feet or stumble? What if it becomes clear that I don't know how to dance? Won't everyone laugh?

The answer to those questions is simple: If you're with the right person, he or she *won't* laugh—and that person's response is the only one that really matters.

If I like a woman, she can step on my feet; in fact, she can stand on them the entire time we dance, or she can just stand there without moving and hold me. It won't make any difference. If she doesn't dance well, we don't need to dance. If she doesn't kiss well, I'll show her how—exuberantly.

That's the key. Exuberance. A person who is eager to please will please despite a million so-called mistakes.

I remember being berated by my prom date for not opening a particular door or not doing some other "expected" thing that anyone with "social graces" should have known. Sure, that made me nervous and uncomfortable. But I was with the wrong girl. There were dozens of girls in my high school who would have given me the leeway to make those mistakes, just happy to be there with me. My fault was not that I made some social mistakes, it was in being with someone who considered those things more important than making me comfortable and having a good time with me.

This concept of making the other person comfortable is crucial. Make that your goal. Take the focus off yourself—and look for someone who seems to think the same way you do.

Go out with a fault-finder, and he or she will find fault. Someone who tries to make others comfortable, on the other hand, will make you comfortable.

The biggest problem people have is thinking that they want what they don't. In other words, a guy may think he wants to go to the prom with the most popular girl in school, when actually, what he really wants is to go with someone who enjoys being with him. Ms. Popularity may have caught his attention and distracted him from his real purpose, making him forget that joy was what he was seeking, not social standing.

This brings me to my main point: Sincere is never wrong. This is one of those rules that is absolutely fundamental. If you don't understand it, your life is destined to be lived at half-staff compared to those who do. So let me repeat it. Sincere is never wrong. It means, simply, that sincere efforts, sincere offers, sincere initiatives toward others are never wrong. If people occasionally respond to your offers with rolled eyes, frowns, or snide remarks, that's *their* problem, not yours.

If you ask someone for a date, and you get anything less than a flattered "thank you"—regardless of whether it is accompanied by a yes or a no—then you are dealing with a jerk. And you should be happy to have learned that so early in your acquaintanceship.

In other words, every sincere offer is a fine thing. Go ahead. Make the offer. There is no "wrong." There is no reason to hold back. Either you will get a very nice response that will be enjoyable for both you and the receiver of your offer, or you will find that you are dealing with a jerk, in which case it makes no difference at all what the response is. What do you care what a jerk does? You can expect a jerk to do something jerky, but so what? You certainly don't want to go through life being governed by the possible negative actions of jerks.

Open up the newspaper. A bank was robbed somewhere. Someone shot someone else. Some workers went on strike. Someone got fired. Someone quit. People argued. People fought.

Things happen. Jerks are *out there.* If your hope is to rid the world of them, you have no time to be reading this book. But most of us who do not hope to rid the world of jerks have realized that we must learn to tune them out, ignore them, and make the best of life while we can.

Once you have decided that you cannot make the world a perfect place and that you cannot rid the world of jerks, you have to decide how *you* are going to live. Will you refuse to go outside because you may run into a jerk? Will you be afraid to ask someone to dance because you may ask a jerk?

Once you see life clearly as it is, you will feel free to make every offer and initiative that occurs to you. The good people in the world will make you feel good for having made those offers and initiatives. And the jerks will try to make you feel bad.

Are you susceptible to their efforts? You shouldn't be. You should have learned by now that they simply must be ignored. For those of us who consider eliminating all the jerks too grand a mission— or too difficult or too scary—we have no other choice. Ignore jerks. Seek out and deal with good people, in business, at dances, on dates, in school.

So, make your efforts. Enjoy them. And enjoy the good responses. Ignore the stupid responses, and keep making your offers.

When you meet that jerk who tries to make you feel foolish for asking, simply refuse to feel foolish. Be proud of your offer and have pity on the person who has not yet learned that a sincere, kind offer has only two classes of possible responses—the sincere thanks that you will get from all good people, and the thousand stupid reactions you may get from the jerks.

A sincere offer is never wrong; and it doesn't hurt at all to waste some on jerks. In fact, only by taking that chance can you sort out and find the good people.

If you think you can go through life being yourself
100 percent of the time and find the right girl who just
happens to like that, you are suffering some grandiose delusions.

For Men Only

If you want a woman to feel loved and comfortable, you have to make her feel as though you understand her. All people want to feel understood, women even more than men. Making them feel understood essentially means sitting down with them once a day and listening and nodding and not voicing your own opinion.

If some women sneak a peek at this, they will think I am cynical, but I am not. I mean this absolutely. And I would advise all of you men to consider your priorities. You want to enjoy women and have them in your life, and to do that you are going to have to make some compromises. If you think you can go through your life being yourself 100 percent of the time, and finding the right girl who just happens to like that, you are suffering some grandiose delusions. The men who get along with women and who get the most enjoyment from them are those who have understood early on that some compromises are crucial. As a result, they made those compromises long ago, they incorporated them into their daily lives and they quit thinking about them, quit complaining to their friends, quit considering that life could be any different from the way it has become for them. Mostly, they have made a commitment to sit and listen and nod, and withhold the urge they used to have to yell, "That's garbage!" or "No way!"

With women, when you voice your opinion at times when they

are trying to be understood, you are merely defeating your own purpose. There are times to argue, sure. But *not* when a woman is trying to be understood. Have your differences over television programs, food, going out or not going out, liking her friends or not liking them, having your friends in or not having them in. All that is "part of the game" so to speak. But once a day, commit yourself to getting quiet, to dropping your opinions out of consideration, and just decide to listen to hers and nod. She may say things you absolutely disagree with, but if this is that one time in the day, change your focus. Get quiet, listen, nod, and—if it's appropriate under the circumstances—hold her.

I don't care what criticisms are leveled at this advice or by whom; it is terrific advice. Because it works. Women will love you for this. You will rise to the very top of the "class" of men, among the one-tenth of one percent who have learned to do this; and you will be appreciated; you will be talked about when women gather; and everyone will envy the woman who has you, because so few of the others' boyfriends or husbands will do anything like this, even though it is *the* one thing most cherished by women.

What if she says things which you find absolutely outlandish? Stupid question. When you decide to go into your understanding/supportive/quiet mode, do it 100 percent. Forget that you are any longer a person with your own ideas and your own opinions. You can be that all day long, you can argue over every tiny detail of life, but when this time comes, don't depart from your course, don't inject an idea here or there. Make sure everything is just pure encouragement to make her feel free to talk on. She will love the game, play it readily, and will rarely demand real responses from you. So it's not that hard to play, as long as you commit yourself entirely and stick to your commitment. Supportive, quiet, nodding, *understanding.*

If you've got this down pat, guys, the rest is gravy.

A Note to Women Who Peeked!

A female editor read this section and strenuously disagreed with what I've said here. She suggested major changes, including the title, "The

Art of Listening." She said that I implied that "women are the only ones who want to be listened to, understood, and comforted" and that "girls or women really don't have anything worthwhile to say, but if guys *pretend* to be listening, it will make girls feel better and they'll be easier to get along with."

Obviously, everyone needs to be listened to, understood, and comforted; and of course women have worthwhile things to say. The implications were intended for a reason. I believe that most guys who are inadequate at listening and communicating aren't going to be very turned on by a title like "The Art of Listening." If you happen to be involved with a guy who doesn't do the things this chapter talks about, I think you would be happy if you could just get him to pretend. I have found that pretending to listen and actually listening aren't really all that different. If you get a guy quiet and get him nodding, you can be sure that some of your points will sink in. Therefore, even at the risk of offending some women who peeked at this "For Men Only" section, I've decided to stick with this advice. If some guys change their behavior for the better, I think most women will be pleased, even if the guys think they've changed for some sneaky, self-serving reason. The same applies to women, of course. It really isn't so sneaky to use some "method" to get along better with someone. Isn't that one goal we all share? If I could get a woman to sit and nod and listen to me once a day, I wouldn't care what her motivations were—I'd enjoy her!

*You will not always win. But with a compliment
and a question you certainly can give
yourself a fighting chance.*

How to Approach Someone
Who Seems Unapproachable

Men constantly see women who they *think* are unapproachable; women feel the same way about many men. Therefore, perhaps the first and primary lesson of this section ought to be: No one is unapproachable. We are all human beings.

That lesson may be comforting to some, but others no doubt will say, "That may look nice in print, but it doesn't work in real life. Sometimes you *do* see someone with whom you know you simply have zero chance."

I understand the feeling. How does a freshman take a junior to the prom? It ain't gonna be easy! I do disagree, however, with that last part: "zero" chance. The chances are always better than zero. You never know what someone else is thinking. You owe it to yourself to at least try. You have to have that "Why-not-go-for-it" attitude.

Perhaps the best way to get the attitude you need is to have a modus operandi you are comfortable with. (By using some big words here, maybe I can confuse you long enough to get you to read on with some hope!) Why not use an approach that acknowledges the distance at the outset—and one that has good features regardless of the outcome. In other words, knowing you have a reasonable, unobtrusive method of approaching, you are much more likely to make an attempt. If your approach is not a lot more than a compliment, of course you should deliver it—for the good of mankind!—and of course it will be accepted and considered.

Okay, so let's set this up: You're at a gathering and someone is there who is gorgeous, a movie star surrounded by attention. Other nationally known celebrities are there; many of them will approach the object of your affection. Does this scenario seem impossible enough? What chance do you have in this situation?

First, you don't have a *good* chance. But you probably have a better chance than you do of, say, winning the lottery. And it costs nothin' to play. It doesn't cost anything. Right? Why not go for it?

Why not wait on the periphery for your movie star to wander away from the crowd? All you need is a chance to get in a few words. What will you say?

"Excuse me, I know you are very busy here, but if you have a minute free this evening or some other time, I would love to talk with you. I really admire your work."

How can that kind of offer get a flat no from any human being? You delivered a very nice compliment, you acknowledged that this person's time is precious, and you didn't ask for much.

Your chances actually are pretty good that the answer will be, "I have a minute now. What do you want to talk about?"

Now you have this person's attention; he or she has asked *you* a question. So, make sure you give a good answer. Another sincere compliment can never be wrong; say that you want to talk about something that obviously takes longer than a minute: "I just wanted to ask you a few questions and try to understand you better. I am so impressed with the way you carry yourself. I wondered about some of the obstacles you have overcome to get to your present level. . . ."

Will anyone try to answer *that* in a minute? Will your movie star give you more time, or suggest that the two of you talk some other time? (Sure, how should you arrange to meet? Should you exchange phone numbers, or set up a date now?)

You will not always win. But with a compliment and a question about the person you are addressing, you certainly can give yourself a fighting chance. Remember, regardless of who you are talking to, he or she is human. And we all have the same favorite subject: ourselves. And one of our favorite "things" is an intelligent, good listener. If you give evidence of being both intelligent and a good listener, you will have value for almost everyone. Will the person you have approached take the time to realize it? Maybe not. That is not your problem.

But if you make no attempt at all, that *is* your problem. If you make a good offer and it is rejected, you can live with that, you can be happy with yourself, and you can approach the next unapproachable person with a fresh batch of confidence.

Good luck. Go for it. Why not?

Consider asking someone to go to a political,
philosophical, literary picnic. What is that? That's just it.
No one knows what it is—but most people want to try
something new if it isn't too scary or dangerous.

How to Ask for a Date—With Confidence

If you are nervous about asking someone for a date, take the pressure off yourself by making the offer unusual or unique. That way, you cannot be compared with anyone else, and your request cannot be considered in the usual way. For example, "Would you like to see the new Spielberg flick Saturday? I saw the previews; it looks pretty interesting."

Really? How interesting can it be? Your potential date has seen dozens, maybe hundreds of movies. How exciting can you make a movie sound? Furthermore, if the movie is good, who wants to sit beside a virtual stranger, nervously wondering whether it's okay to laugh at certain jokes or react naturally? Asking someone to go to a movie puts all the pressure on you, and gives you little opportunity to distinguish yourself. The date almost depends on how good the movie is; and even if it is good, it is likely to be a somewhat strained experience.

A Political, Philosophical, Literary Picnic

On the other hand, consider asking someone to attend a political, philosophical, literary picnic. What is *that*? That is just the point.

No one knows what it is—so it cannot be compared with anything else. If your potential date has any typical human curiosity, he or she will probably want to go. Most people want to try something new, if it isn't too scary or dangerous. So, what if you're asked, "What's a political, philosophical, literary picnic?" What then?

"Come and find out." It's a bit of politics (you're going to read some things out of the paper), it's a bit of philosophy (you're going to explain some thoughts you have), and it's a bit literary (you're going to read a story or two).

Nearly everyone likes to have a story read to them—especially if it happens to be good, and even more so if the person was fortunate enough to have grown up with adults around who read to him or her. Most parents realize that the best way to start educating children is to expose them to books early. Bedtime stories have been one of the most valued aspects of the parent-child bond since ancient times. So why not take advantage of the bond that reading together can create? Take your date to some quiet place—your house or a field or under a tree somewhere or near some water—and read. Select seven or eight short passages, so that if one is boring, another may be more stimulating. That takes the pressure off, and makes variety the essential experience. You are free, of course, like a solo guitarist, to offer a few of your own thoughts before and after each reading. Add a pretzel or two, a box of Kentucky Fried Chicken, and you have it all—refreshments, entertainment, originality.

If you have found a relaxing and comfortable place, you can't possibly go wrong. If you happen to be with a person who groans the whole time and says how stupid your "picnic" is, you are with an A-Number-One-Dud-Zip-Zero. And you will be glad to have discovered that so soon. How are you ever going to enjoy someone who is bored by relaxing exposure to new ideas?

Go ahead! What do you have to lose?

What you have to gain is a friend who finds you unique, different, interesting—and it's easy to become attracted to someone you see in this way. So, why not let Hemingway, Twain, and Shakespeare work for you? Almost anyone can listen attentively to a story for a few minutes, knowing that a great story may not start fast, and that the threads of a great story may interweave subtly. Not every story, not even among the classics, produces thunder and lightning in the opening line. But most people like stories—in the right setting—and will be challenged to listen attentively and to think about them.

The point is, a political, philosophical, literary picnic like that is good entertainment; and it is *not* a typical date. Be different. Be incomparable. Think up your own unusual ideas. When was the last time you invited someone to go out hunting for smooth, flat rocks? That's part one of your date. If you both have fun, continue with part two, going to a lake or riverbank and skipping the stones in the water.

There are few things more enjoyable than being with someone you like at sunset by some quiet lake, with a hundred flat rocks at your side just waiting to skip through the water, sending ever-widening concentric waves to the end of the universe and back. If you haven't tried it yet, then truly the best is yet to come for you.

If you live in a place where the gathering of flat rocks would not give away your stone-skipping plans, then all the better. Make the most of the rock-gathering expedition, and keep secret what the rocks are for—you know the value of secrets.

What other unusual ideas can you come up with? If you have any great ones, let me know.

Hints won't do it. Most of us are too thick!

Women: Take Two Giant Steps

Women often seem to lament the fact that they have to wait around to be asked to this or that, while men, they think, are lucky. Men get to do the asking.

I want to add just one thought to that. Men don't feel nearly as lucky in that position as women seem to think they do. Most men (even those of us who pretend to be confident most of the time!) are very shy about having to ask. It never gets truly easy putting yourself out and being open to rejection. Some men learn to do it better than others, but I've never met anyone who enjoyed it, or who was as casual about rejection as we all try to pretend to be.

What this means is that women could often take giant steps ahead in getting what they want, or in getting the men they want, by letting their feelings be known. Hints won't do it. Most of us are too thick! Or too shy. We don't catch hints nearly as well as we should. That means you may have to make your interest absolutely clear. If you don't want to actually ask a man for a date, it wouldn't hurt to tell him that, if he asked you, you would *not* say no. (Even that might confuse him. Tell him you would say *yes!*)

You don't have to extend yourself excessively. You could say you've been wondering what he would be like on a date. . . . You could say you've been wondering why he has never asked you. You could ask if he is planning to ask you out before Christmas, or before the end of the school year, or before the end of high school, or before the much-awaited Vernal Equinox (whatever that is).

I just think women could make things a lot easier for everyone—and still do the asking or hinting discreetly, so that indicating their interest doesn't say more than they mean it to.

"I've always wondered what it would be like going out with you." That would be something every man would like to hear and be able to respond to. It wouldn't give him a big head, like he suddenly had you wrapped around his finger. It would just make him realize that he could get a *yes* by asking you.

I sure would like to know I could get a yes before having to go through the task of asking for a date. I think almost every man would agree.

How to Kiss and Make Love

Some people will turn to a section with a title like this and expect to find diagrams or photos of "proper" positions or special techniques. I know that when I was struggling to grow up, that's precisely what I was looking for. I was also worried about nearly everything, although I didn't feel I could ask anyone about the things I wanted to know. For example: How do you kiss? Is your mouth open or closed? Do your teeth ever hit? Is it nose to nose or do you have to tilt your head? Who tilts which way?

The questions didn't stop with kissing. How do you hold hands—do you interwine fingers, or grip the whole hand, all four fingers together? How do you dance close? Are there steps you have to do? Is everyone just shuffling around out there, or are they doing something? Do you always rotate in the same direction? If not, how often do you shift directions? How do you "wiggle" on a dance floor so you don't look stupid? Is it okay to look around while you're slow dancing, or should you close your eyes? Is it okay to smile, or do you have to look serious? Can you stare at the girl you're dancing with if she looks terrific? How often should you look around or spin around or look away or look at her or look at your own feet?

As you can imagine, it got even worse for me with love-making. How do you know when it's "time"? How do you know if it's okay to touch your partner in a certain place? What if it seems time to make love but your body isn't "ready"? How "ready" do you have to be? Should you keep your eyes open or closed? Do you have to "sneak a peak" or can you just stare? Is it okay to talk?

Some of you are reading these questions thinking, "What a jerk!" while others are wondering about the answers. Typically, people have all sorts of "dumb" questions, even people who have considerable experience and supposedly should know everything.

What's the point? I truly wish I had understood the point many years ago, so I would not have made so many mistakes, so I would not have spent so much time worrying and being self-conscious, so I would not have marred my enjoyment and my lovers' by wondering if I was doing something wrong or if I was being compared with someone else who did something different or better.

If I have learned one thing, it is that there are no right answers. The right answer for one person may be the wrong answer for someone else. Just when you think you know how to please the opposite sex, you may find someone who requires a completely different kind of approach or attention or interaction.

What does this mean for you? It means that every time two people meet who have an interest in kissing or making love or any of the steps in between, the event should be looked upon as nothing less than an adventure, a new journey to discovery, a kind of wonderful exploration. Because everyone is different, there is no right and wrong.

If you find someone who likes you, who wants to be kissed by you, you can't possibly make a mistake. Say you kiss in some way that that person doesn't particularly like. So what? He or she will appreciate that you want to kiss, and the two of you can fumble around enjoyably until you find a better method.

The same applies to the whole process. With the right person, everything is negotiable, changeable.

It always reminds me of fashion, strangely enough. Imagine seeing someone you don't like wearing a red shirt and purple slacks. You may think it looks awful. Yet, see your favorite person wearing that same shirt and tie, and suddenly it's "cool." Put Christie Brinkley in any old sack, torn jeans, or red plaids against orange stripes, and I'll still think she looks terrific.

In other words, if you do something that brings derisive laughter, you are simply with the wrong person. Amused laughter, of course, is different. You should be able to enjoy that together. You are not going to do everything perfectly. But that doesn't matter. If a person likes you, most of your "mistakes" will be endearing, almost charming, particularly if your intentions are clearly good.

No one who likes you is going to be bothered by any kind of mistake or style or manner of doing something. Whereas you will not be able to please someone who does not like you, regardless of what you do.

So, to go back to the beginning: How *do* you kiss and make love? With wide-eyed eagerness and enthusiasm, and with one purpose: to express your special feelings to the person you are kissing or making love with. If that person shares your special feelings and is eager to return them, you *cannot* make a mistake. You can do some things that you may wish to correct or alter in some way, but there will be no mistakes. There will only be the joy of mutual discovery and exploration.

If your kissing or your love-making don't feel like joyous explorations free of worry, then reconsider who you are kissing or making love with. *That* is the only mistake you really have to worry about: being with or making love with someone who is not eagerly feeling the same as you.

Once you are with someone who shares your goal—to express special feelings and to make the other person feel good—there is only success ahead. Just relax and enjoy!

Do You Have the Right Equipment?

Before concluding this section, I want to talk about "equipment"— about bodies, breasts, and penises.

Every woman I have ever known has over-estimated the degree of men's interest in breasts. Sure, men talk about breasts, tell jokes, say they love 'em huge, etc., but in reality, men have only a minor attraction to them. In other words, all sorts of men (even men who claim to be "breast men") are perfectly happy with small-breasted or flat-chested women.

The size of a woman's breasts actually means very little. Often times men feel more masculine with a woman with small breasts, because they get a chance to make the woman feel whole and complete and fine just as she is.

Ironically, even women with very ample breasts usually think they are too small. Only women with extemely large breasts feel otherwise, and they are often unhappy that their breasts are so large. They say their breasts get in the way of jogging and sports, and they often claim their breasts attract too much attention, making it difficult to get a true reading of a man's intentions since his concentration initially seems so centered on their breasts.

In a nutshell, there is hardly a woman in the world who thinks her breasts are just right, and yet there are hardly any men who really care. Sure, men love "big tits" when girl-watching at the beach. But for a mate, or even for a date, the size of a woman's breasts is not at all important.

Men have a similar problem with the size of their muscles and particularly with the size of their penises. In one respect, men are lucky. Women can't see at a glance what size their penises are. But men nevertheless often feel self-conscious and worry, particularly when love-making becomes a possibility, what women will think of their penises. "Will she suddenly be less interested in me when she discovers how small my penis is?"

Again, the major point is, nearly everyone shares these fears to some extent. Yet, when you find someone who likes you, the size of this or that body part becomes unimportant. I have never heard any woman say the bigger the penis, the greater her enjoyment. Sexuality is more mental than physical, you might say. Find someone who likes you and wants to make you feel good, and he or she won't care what size your breasts are or what size your penis is. So don't waste your time worrying. There are many attractive men and women who will be attracted to you precisely as you are. Better to spend your time finding them than worrying about being perfect for everyone. If you do come across someone who makes fun of your small breasts or small penis, rest assured that you have found a very insecure person who has a bigger problem than you do. Secure people appreciate differences. It is only insecure people who feel threatened and who may seek to lift their own self-image (temporarily) by making fun of others.

*Surprise people with good news, with suggestions
or ideas they will be happy to hear.
But if you suspect that what you are about to say will
have a negative impact, be willing to add a preface.*

How to Make an Agreement that Can Add Harmony and Maturity to a Relationship

If a relationship is subject to fits of sudden anger for no real reason, with sudden accusations flung in the air, it is not a very enjoyable relationship, and probably won't last very long.

But a pattern like this can be reversed, and harmony and maturity encouraged, through one simple agreement that two people ought to be willing to make to each other: Never surprise your friend or partner (or anyone you care about) with a problem or negative feeling.

Surprise people with little gifts, with good news, with suggestions or ideas they will be happy to hear. But if you suspect that what you are about to say will have a negative impact on them, be willing to add a preface.

In other words, introduce, warn, prepare, and then *ask for permission* to bring up the thing that is bothering you.

"Pat, there is something which has been bothering me that I would like to discuss with you. Do you have time now to lend me your patience and understanding?"

You may look at the above question and think right away, "Gawd, I would never say something like that." But if you would not, you should also be willing to look in the mirror and say, "Gawd, am I ever immature"—because you are.

No matter what your age, you ought to want to conduct yourself in a mature or at least an intelligent way. You should at least strive to add harmony to your relationships, rather than being content to just use people as "data dumps."

Be assured that it is difficult to maintain attraction in an atmosphere where harmony is not a goal. If you persist in feeling that you simply have to spew out what is on your mind, you deserve the problems you will inevitably have.

When you decide, however, that you want harmony, that you want to get along better with someone, you will make an effort to live up to the "agreement," even if the other person occasionally fails. Surprise with good news, but introduce, warn, prepare, and *ask for permission,* for the right time, to bring up bad news.

If you find yourself getting upset because you are trying to follow this formula but your friend—or arguing partner—is not, then mention the agreement, again and again if necessary, but not in the middle of a squabble. Wait until you are getting along fine, and then introduce, warn, prepare, and ask. Say that you would like to maintain the kind of positive mutual feelings you are experiencing at that time, and that you want to apologize for *your* past failures to apply the formula to the relationship. If you are with a good person, he or she will likely see the wisdom of this method of getting along, and will offer to adopt its requirements as well.

If your special person insists on dumping data anytime he or she feels like it, you have a decision to make. Do you want to stay involved with someone who is not committed to harmony and intelligence? Relationships are rarely problem-free, even when both participants are making a real effort to live intelligently and considerately. But when one of the two is not even trying to do this, the chances of having a satisfying relationship plummet.

It simply doesn't make sense to spend too much time with someone who is willing to mar your good mood any old time for any old reason.

In any relationship, the two people involved should try to uplift each other whenever possible. It is not sufficient to claim you are "just being yourself." A relationship requires more than just yourself. It requires your best self, your best foot forward.

If you have been justifying your actions with the meager phrase "that's just the way I am" or "that's just how I feel," it's time for you to rethink life, liberty, and the pursuit of happiness. You can get away with that way of thinking provided you go to live on a desert island. But if you are living with others—with parents, friends, or that "special someone"—more is required of you. Harmony and intelligence and maturity demand that you be a bit better than "just yourself"; that you withhold some negative feelings and ideas; that you have some patience and restraint; that you make a personal commitment, despite the inevitable failings of others, to *try* to uplift those around you—especially those you care about, or those with whom you must interact regularly—rather than bring them down.

You won't get an A for this on any report card; it may be that no one ever notices or acknowledges this mature, intelligent commitment. But your life will be better for it—and so will the lives of those around you.

If the people around you do not do this already, teach them—gently. Introduce, warn, prepare, and ask. Or just show them this section and get them thinking. It is to everyone's advantage to promote harmony and intelligent living, rather than to be victimized constantly, unexpectedly, by whatever whims or feelings happen to cross someone else's mind.

Remember how you felt when you initially made the effort to turn a stranger into a special friend? You liked something in that person, believed that sharing would add a special flavor to your life. Chances are it did, and that it would again, if you let it.

Remember Why You Started

I am often amazed that both "halves" of a couple lose sight of why they originally got involved in the relationship.

Being single or alone is not the worst thing in the world. As a matter of fact, it really isn't bad at all. You can read, watch television, go to fairs, parks, and malls. You can do all sorts of things, yet most of these things seem as though they would be more enjoyable *shared.*

But the next thing you know, in too many cases, the only things being shared are arguments, usually over little, inconsequential things.

What time did you get home? Who were you with? Who did the dishes last? Who left that towel on the floor?

Oh sure, there are problems to be solved between two people, and there always will be. But probably *the* most important thing to remember is why you got started in the first place. Remember how you felt when you initially made the effort to turn a stranger into a special friend? You liked something about that person. You believed that sharing would add a special flavor to your life. Chances are it did, and that it would again, if you let it.

When I was going to school at Duke University, there were times when I was not particularly happy with the basketball situation. The coach and I didn't get along, I didn't like our style of play, I didn't like certain other things that were happening. Yet it was tremendously useful to keep reminding myself how much I had dreamed of playing college basketball, how hard I had strived, how many hours I had practiced.

Would I throw away all that past by being disgruntled and going through the motions once I had achieved what I had sought for so long and worked so hard toward? When I thought of it that way, giving up didn't make sense. It *is* possible to put negative aspects of a situation aside and dwell on the positive, remembering the good things and the reasons you worked to get where you are.

Naturally, if you are in a relationship that is not good for you, you should get out of it. Make a quick, clean break and go on with your life. But while you are in a relationship, don't sabotage it with garbage, with pettiness and unnecessary gripes and whines and aches and pains.

Remember the joy you experienced when you first made that relationship happen—and make it keep happening by giving it your best shot.

Remembering the past, in cases like this, can help to propel you toward the future.

5

Using Hypnosis for Success In Sports, Dieting, and Habit-Formation

Many people are frightened away from hypnosis by
misconceptions, television showmanship, and science fiction.
But hypnosis is recognized and used by the
American Medical Association. It is safe and useful,
and it can be terrific.
I invite you to see for yourself.

Does Hypnosis Really Work?

Hypnosis is so natural, so effortless, and in a way, so everyday and commonplace, that it is difficult to believe that anything is happening at all.

Even when I was successfully hypnotizing my mother when she was dying of cancer, I still did not have real assurance that anything was really happening. I suspected she was telling me that I was making her feel better just to make *me* feel better. Or I thought maybe she actually *thought* she felt better, though again, nothing was really happening to her physically.

What I am saying is that even a hypnotist has doubts. Even a hypnotist, or someone who has already enjoyed some benefits from hypnosis, still wonders about what really happens. Does something actually take place? Something marvelous? Or is it "all in the mind"? Naturally, when you are using a process that "plays" with the mind, you stretch the typical meaning of the phrase "all in the mind," and that, too, is confusing. It's like thinking about thinking. The farther you take it, the more confusing it gets.

So let me admit from the outset, I have had my doubts. Am I really qualified to hypnotize people and claim I can help them?

Several things have enabled me to answer that question yes. First, I was helping people—regularly. I was hypnotizing individuals and groups, and people were coming back to me saying I helped them.

When my mother was ill, I began to doubt what I was doing (actually, I was hoping a "real" hypnotist could do even more) so I took her to an AMA-certified physician who used hypnosis, who told me that I was doing exactly the same thing he did in his practice. He then went on to try his way of doing it, but with fewer successful results than I was getting.

Though I had worked with my mother and with many others, I still was not sure something was *really* happening—until one day at an airport.

I was sitting alone, at the gate—no one was within fifty feet of me—and I decided to hypnotize myself. I went through my normal process and had no awareness of anything being any different from any other time. I relaxed, I visualized, I "journeyed" to the hypnotic state, and I made several hypnotic suggestions. Then I brought myself out of it. I had conducted no amazing tests, I had not eaten any onions and thought they were apples, nor had I recalled any deep dark secrets.

I did, however, wake up to the sudden realization that I was completely surrounded by stewardesses—not twenty or thirty feet away, and not just two or three of them. Nine or ten stewardesses were beside me, holding various animated conversations, and it was obvious that they were not paying much attention to me. They merely assumed I was in a deep sleep, and they were ignoring me completely by the time I awoke. Several of them were close enough for me to touch. One was sitting right next to me, only inches away. The point is, at no time did I have even a shred of recognition of their presence. They were talking loudly; some were lovely, and I—usually a very interested bachelor—had no awareness whatever of any change in my surroundings.

I opened my eyes and looked around in disbelief. I never would have guessed that I could sleep that soundly even in the middle of the night, to say nothing of being that deeply in a trance. To me this was awesome evidence of something special going on; indeed, it was the surest proof I'd had of a highly concentrated state of thought or of a successful journey into the depths of the mind. I was exhilarated.

I had hypnotized myself, and others, for a couple of years, had done some tricks and, as I have said, even removed some pain, but through all that, I would not have guessed that I could ever do anything to myself that would make me totally oblivious to nine or ten pretty women surrounding me in an airport. It showed me the power that hypnosis can have. And it is that power that I want to share with you—for whatever uses you find important in your life.

I mention this story only to let you know that it is normal—indeed, healthy—to doubt. But for a while, try merely to have some faith. Do it—even if you suspect that nothing is happening. Maybe nothing *is* happening. Maybe your suspicions will be right. But of course, what do you have to lose by trying, and by relaxing and filling your mind with positive thoughts every day?

You have nothing to lose, and a new life to gain. I bet that you'll find out that something strange and wonderful is happening. You have the ability to tap a useful and exhilerating power you never knew you had.

Hocus-Pocus: Misconceptions About Hypnosis

There are a lot of misconceptions about hypnosis—what it is and what it can do—largely because of stage-show hypnotists who use certain aspects of the hypnotic process to entertain and amaze audiences. Most everyone is familiar with hypnotized subjects who have barked like a dog on stage or have eaten an apple and cried real tears after being told suddenly that it was an onion.

Because of the popular misconceptions perpetuated by such things, people have all sorts of fears that they need not have. "When I am under hypnosis, can someone tell me I am a bird and make me jump out of a window?"

No, no one can do that to you. You need not have any fears about negative aspects of hypnosis. There is an easy way to assure that everything you ever hear under hypnosis will benefit you, and every good hypnotist uses this safeguard in one form or another to make his or her clients comfortable with the very positive process of hypnosis.

The Safeguard

Before you are ever hypnotized, you should go over the whole process and become thoroughly familiar with what will happen, so that there will be no surprises.

The first suggestion that any good hypnotist will give you under hypnosis will usually be something like this: "You are now entering into a hypnotic state. You know this process well and you know what it can do for you—but if at any time you hear something that is not in keeping with the process we have discussed, you will wake up immediately and the hypnotic trance will end."

That beginning should put you at ease and make you realize that there will be no surprises. You will become thoroughly familiar with what is about to be said—on tape or by the hypnotist—and any deviation from that will stop everything. That way you can be sure that no hypnotist can make you do anything against your will. (It would be difficult, if not impossible, anyway, but this way there's no doubt at all.) The hypnotist's task is to do your will and nothing else. He or she finds what it is that *you* want and helps you to get just that and nothing else. (With a cassette tape, there is no fear of surprises or of the unknown, which is precisely the reason cassettes can be more effective than a session with a hypnotist.)

Magic and Potential Fulfillment

Hypnosis is not magic, but often it seems like it, especially to subjects who have tried—and failed—to "cure" themselves of an ailment, a habit, or a fear through willpower. They often feel there must be some magic in a process that enables them to do something that they couldn't do on their own.

When people fulfill a potential by accomplishing something, they usually feel euphoric about it. It's great to do your best, to feel yourself making progress, to be doing things you couldn't do before.

Hypnosis can help you to get these great feelings—so in that way, hypnosis *is* magic.

The Wrong Worries and the Real Question

Most people about to enter on a program of hypnosis find themselves worrying and wondering, "Will it work?"

This is normal. If you have tried a hundred times to stop biting your nails for example, and each time you soon failed to uphold your commitment, you are naturally going to doubt that there will suddenly be a simple way to stop, regardless of what some doctor or hypnotist or author says.

Nevertheless, the big question is *not* "Will it work?" but instead, "Will you set aside the time to *make* it work?"

The process *will* work. It has worked thousands of times in circumstances more difficult than yours, and it can work for you. If it doesn't work, most likely that will not be because the process failed, but because *you* failed to set aside the time to let the process succeed.

So, if you are still filled with doubt about whether this hypnotic business can really help *you,* do yourself one favor now. Commit yourself to giving your time. If you give the process time, it will succeed. Accept this now on faith; give it a chance until you have time to see for yourself. Hypnosis, properly used, works on just about anyone. Most likely, it can work for you.

What Kind of Problems Can Hypnosis Deal With?

As I have already said, hypnosis is not magic. It cannot cure you of cancer, and it cannot make poison ivy go away. What it can do, very effectively, is deal with problems that have a definite mental aspect and involve willpower, nervousness, fear, or bad habits. Hypnosis is extremely effective at enabling people to stop biting nails, to stop smoking cigarettes, to stop overeating, to start and continue exercise programs, to overcome excessive fears of dogs, heights, darkness, flying, failure, and so on.

Hypnosis has helped many athletes to perform at their best by freeing their minds, taking away the doubts, worries, and fears that interrupt a fluid golf stroke, a proper pitching motion, or a smooth backhand.

Hypnosis cannot usually turn a mediocre player into a star, but it can help a player to live up to star potential by allaying fears and other mentally based hindrances of player performance.

Whim Power, Willpower, and the Power of Hypnosis

It is easy, when you are sitting in an air-conditioned room, to make a decision to start some grand new program. "I am going to run fifty wind-sprints every day," you can say, as you sip a soda, and pull open a bag of potato chips. That's a whim, a nice thought, something you would *like* to do but not really something you have resolved to do. You would *like* to be a pilot, a journalist, a senator, a coach, and a doctor too, but you probably have not resolved to *become* any of those things.

Many of those great professions will be forgotten along the way, just the way you will forget the fifty wind-sprints once you get out on the field and do seven and find you're out of breath, your legs are tired, and you're thinking how enjoyable another soda would be.

Sitting in your room, your whim was to do fifty sprints a day, just as on the field your whim is to drink a soda—but in this instance, of course, you'll walk off the field and get the soda, because you have merely pitted one whim against another. *When you pit whim against whim, the most immediate whim will win.*

It sounds like a tongue-twister, but it is a good point to remember.

You would be foolish to walk off the field frustrated at your lack of willpower when the whole time you were dealing with mere whim power. When you're cool and rested, you decide *it would be nice* to get into great shape. But then when you're hot, tired, and parched you decide it would be nice to be sipping a soda inside. Both seem like very intelligent decisions under the circumstances—and both are, so no frustration should result.

We are smart to do the things our minds tell us to do. This is basic. If we put our hands in a flame, our minds say, *"Ow!* Remove them!" If we walk near the edge of a steep cliff, our minds tell us, "Get back!" Learning to follow our minds often makes good sense.

But sometimes we ask ourselves about what our mind is telling us—and *why*. Where does the mind get its information? And can that information be changed?

If you want to stay on the field and run those fifty wind-sprints because it is important to get in shape for a big race, then you may be stepping out of the whim stage and into the *will* stage.

True willpower easily overcomes whim power. Whim power, remember, is a fleeting, "it would be nice" type of thought. But willpower is an ardent desire, a fervent hope backed by a realistic plan. Willpower is a thought turned into a definite want or even into an almost desperate need.

For example, overweight people often say, "I would *like* to be slim. I am going on a diet. I would *like* to lose fifty pounds." But they also just love to gulp down milkshakes and devour whole bags of potato chips and cookies. "Just love" is a key phrase. Because, when you really look at the likes and dislikes of such people, they really would rather *eat* than be slim. Naturally, they would like both. But when forced to choose between the two, they really desire the pleasure of eating more than they desire the pleasure of being slim. Their diets fail, of course, because they have that choice constantly and, listening to what their minds tell them, they choose to eat most of the time. They do not diet because they have never taken slimness out of the "would be nice" category and put it into the "just love" category. They could spend their whole lives thinking they have no willpower, when really their minds are merely choosing an immediate whim over a more distant one.

If a person really wants to diet, or to do fifty wind-sprints every day, that wish has to be transformed into a true desire. And there are few easier ways to achieve that than through hypnosis.

The Crucial Quiet Period

In every form of self-help or self-realization, the most important transformations take place in a quiet place, where you are removed from the environment in which you developed some bad habit or some behavior that needs changing. In hypnosis, this quiet period is also the focal point of positive change. You have to make time for yourself to get away, to disappear from your normal, everyday world.

There is no precise blueprint, however, for what getting away means to you. Some people can get away in the midst of a busy hotel lobby or airport—simply by closing their eyes and tuning out everything around them. Others need to stroll by the seaside, stare into a fire, walk in the woods, or sit by a stream.

You may be able to get away by lying under your bed—a place you normally never go—or by sitting in a dark room or going into a closet. It may be enough to just go into your bedroom and lock the door. How you get away depends solely on you. Find what is best for you, but remember, the quiet period is crucial. You need to commit yourself to it.

In addition, a certain ritual may be useful to help you get into the right frame of mind.

Rituals

Nearly all religions use rituals to help create atmospheres that make their teachings seem more forceful. Whether they include rain dances and war paint, steaming cauldrons and witches' brew, or chanting and a special environment, rituals help to make the whole process more significant, more profound, and therefore more long-lasting in the minds of the participants. In hypnosis, too, a special environment and ritual—perhaps simply a candlelit room and some classical music—may be beneficial.

Imprinting

The purpose of a ritual and the crucial quiet period is to imprint deeply on your mind the new information you want to give it. You don't give your mind this new information during a television commercial, or just before falling asleep at night. Doing so during these times won't hurt, of course, but it isn't likely to make the given information stick the way it will if the circumstances are more carefully prepared.

Hypnosis is merely a process whereby you create the best possible circumstances for reprogramming your mind, so that your inner mind begins giving you suggestions you want to hear, such as, "Stay on the field; you can do fifty wind-sprints," or, "Relax, you don't need to go back to the refrigerator. You want to be slim; you can do it."

Through hypnosis you can reach your inner mind. You will suddenly find it easy to do things that before were difficult, because the inner voice is no longer in conflict with your wants.

What Happens During Hypnosis

Imagine that someone suddenly walked up to you, grabbed you, tied you up, and forced you to sit in a chair for ten hours where there wasn't room to stand up, stretch out your arms, or to straighten your legs. It would seem like a terrible punishment. The ten hours would drag on like years and it would be difficult for you to think of anything but your discomfort and the clock—until the time was over.

But if instead that same someone had said, "You have just won a free trip to Europe," that same cramped ten-hour sitting position in a 747 would have a completely different meaning. It might actually be quite enjoyable.

You have undoubtedly heard the statement, "It's all in your mind," many times. And it's true quite often. The way you *think* about things is the way things *are*. And it's more than that.

The Two Yous

Your mind functions on several levels. On one level you can be watching television, while some other part of your mind is sorting out sounds—ignoring birds and crickets and radios, waiting for a honking horn or a knock on the door. You are not even aware of all the sounds being sorted out but inside your brain, some part of you is listening.

You see the multiple-functioning of the mind clearly with dieters. Most of us are familiar with a friend or family member (or ourselves!) who will walk to the refrigerator saying, "I know I shouldn't eat anymore but. . . ."

These people would like to lose weight, but they would like to eat, too. You could probably think of dozens of other times when you recognize that you have two (or more) distinct desires: "I want this but I want that." You feel both of them conflicting. It is as though two separate people are at work in you.

Hypnosis is a means of coordinating your wants so that both yous want the same thing and are not in conflict. It enables the inner you to want the same things as the outer you.

Do you want to lose weight or do you want to eat? The question is, which do you really want more? To be successful at dieting, you have to convince your inner self that you would rather be slim than eat.

How does hypnosis do that?

Hypnosis reaches the inner part of you, and reprograms it to want what the outer you wants. The mind, it seems, runs like a computer or a tape recorder. Whatever goes into it is what comes out of it. Dieters, for example, say they want to lose weight, but their minds are programmed with the knowledge that eating is enjoyable. Think back on your own eating history. When you were an infant and you got hungry, you cried and suddenly someone stuck a bottle in your mouth and you were happy. Such reinforcement continued with candy, ice cream, cake, and cookies. You were crying and unhappy, and food made you happy. Eating, of course, is a pleasurable activity. So when you are unhappy or depressed about something, your inner mind seeks out some compensating, pleasurable activity. It doesn't take into account the reason for your unhappiness or depression. It just recognizes your displeasure and offers some pleasure. It says, "Hey, c'mon, chin up, get something to eat, that's fun."

Of course fat people will never lose weight until they teach— or reprogram—their minds not to offer their bodies food as a solution to problems.

Reprogramming

How do you reprogram your inner mind? You talk to it. You tell it over and over again what you want. Remember the tape recorder?

You've built up a whole library of "food is good" cassettes, so you need to tape over those. Replace those tapes with ones saying, "slim is good, slim makes me happy."

How does the inner mind get programmed and reprogrammed? It just seems to pick up what it is exposed to over a period of time. It seems normally to be a rather slow learner. It is very willing to change, but you can't change a slow learner overnight. Remember, over a period of time it "records" a lot of information. To reprogram it, you have to tape over all of that information. You either have to do that by exposing it to new ideas over a long period of time, or exposing it dynamically, profoundly, over a shorter period. Regardless of how you do it, though, you can't tape over many cassettes in one day.

Recording

You don't usually know when your mind is recording. It seems to slip in and out of the recording mode constantly, picking up a little of this and a little of that. Therefore, logically, it ends up with whatever it is exposed to most often.

Scientifically or physiologically, this recording process is explained by brain-wave frequencies. In a normal waking state, the brain emits a certain measurable wave. But at certain times the brain emits different waves.

During sleep, brain waves block out a lot of activity that normally enters your consciousness. Your brain is still functioning of course—it hears wake-up alarms, loud noises, and who knows what else—but it does not take in as much as when you are awake.

There are also different waves and frequencies at certain times while you are awake. For instance just before you fall asleep, just after you wake up, sometimes when you are driving or day-dreaming—usually when you are particularly relaxed—your mind slips into a different frequency.

This relaxation frequency is the one we are concerned with in hypnosis, because this frequency is most useful for reaching the inner mind and reprogramming it.

Hypnosis is nothing more than a method of calling up or bringing about that special state of relaxation, that special brain-wave frequency, *when you want it,* so that mental programming or reprogramming becomes purposeful and sustained, not left to chance over a period of time.

Imagine that your brain is like photographic film. If you leave the shutter of the camera open, you can record many impressions over a period of time. And when developed, the photograph won't look like anything recognizable because so many things have been imprinted. But by using a camera, you press a button and *zip*! you record just at that one instant, and therefore get a clear picture.

The hypnotic process is like a camera. It allows you to reach your inner film and record in a short period of time, clearly and vividly, what otherwise would be a confusing jumble created by long-time exposure and by frequency slips at various, random times.

The hypnotic process brings about the altered brain-wave frequency that permits you to reach that inner mind and make clear pictures in place of what is already there.

The DJ Plays the Hits

Don't forget that your inner recorder is large. It contains a whole library of cassettes, you might say. You can reach it by hypnosis, but you can't change everything immediately.

Like you, the disc jockey of your inner recorder most often tends to play the most recently acquired cassettes—so your hypnotic "taping over" will often work for you. However, there are also oldies to contend with. If you want to do a thorough job of changing the music, you have to program often—until you get the DJ to play only what you want to hear.

At first you will have to call the request line frequently to remind the DJ in your mind, but the more programmed tapes he or she has (the tapes *you* have provided), the more of them will be played. If you call often and tape over all of the cassettes with your "favorite songs," the DJ will have to play *your* music. And that is what hypnosis is all about—getting that inner DJ to play what you really want to hear. The DJ will do it if the mind is programmed often enough for it. The DJ plays what is there, what is most often requested—the hits. And *your* calls determine what's hot.

The Process of Hypnotizing

The hypnotic process, regardless of whether it's brought about by a hypnotist or by a cassette, uses a series of simple, very natural steps. You may be surprised, perhaps even disappointed, to learn that hypnosis does not require a swinging watch on a chain or a rotating disk that you stare into, and that you will not suddenly be sent into some strange hallucinogenic trance.

Each step is (almost disappointingly) natural. The steps are: (1) commitment/disappearance, (2) progressive physical relaxation, (3) mental relaxation/envisioning, (4) induction, (5) imprinting, and (6) withdrawal. Let's look at each of these.

Commitment/Disappearance

Most books on hypnosis don't call this a step at all, but I think it may be the most important, because most people have a great deal of difficulty suddenly stopping their lives and their trains of thought in order to disappear for half an hour into another world. They want to hurry through each step, condense the process down to a couple of minutes, and perhaps even get in a few other thoughts they've been wanting to consider but just haven't had time for.

But like most things, if you're going to do it halfway and give it only a partial effort, you're doomed to getting, at best, partial results.

When you decide to put aside a half-hour for hypnosis, make a complete commitment. Go to a place where you know you won't be interrupted (lock yourself away if necessary) and then tell yourself something like this:

"Now I am going to go through the process of hypnosis. I am setting aside this time for my personal benefit, and I am going to give it my complete attention for the next half hour. I am not going to accomplish anything else in the next half hour, so I might just as well put aside all other thoughts and give myself fully to this. I will pick up my other concerns later, but for now, I will concentrate only on this."

If you have particularly persistent thoughts that don't seem to want to go away, stop the hypnotic process and write down the thoughts you wish to resume when the hypnotic process is over. Oftentimes the act of putting them on paper is all your mind needs to let them go for the time needed for hypnosis. Some deep, slow breathing at the outset may also help you to make a complete break with the world around you and thus help you to achieve deeper, more effective hypnosis.

Progressive Physical Relaxation

To make your mind responsive to imprinting, it is usually best to begin by relaxing the body. You can do this simply by lying down on the floor or in bed, and progressively relaxing each muscle in your body, beginning with your toes and working your way up through your feet, calves, knees, thighs, stomach, and so on.

Often it helps to begin the process by flexing or tightening each muscle, or all of your muscles at once, so that you can feel a very definite sensation of relaxation as soon as you begin.

Once you begin the relaxation process, it is helpful to imagine your body as a dry, hard sponge, with hoses attached to your toes that gradually let water flow into your body, making it progressively more supple, saturated, and relaxed. You can almost see the water flowing up through your body, relaxing you more and more as the water continues to flow.

Occasionally you will feel the urge to move because some part of your body may be brushing against the floor or against a blanket in some uncomfortable way. You can move in this case, but it is probably better to learn to "direct the water" to the place of discomfort and let the body become relaxed internally. When you begin, you may find it difficult to lie perfectly still. But after you do it several times, you will get more and more confident in your ability to "think away" discomfort rather than having to toss and turn to get comfortable.

Of course, you are not compelled to use the water-sponge method. You may imagine yourself as a chalk-drawn body on a blackboard gradually being erased. Or you may use any other mental picture that appeals to you and helps aid your relaxation process. Most people do find that some form of mental imagining helps them to relax.

Since this is only a preliminary step along the way to hypnosis, you may tend to hurry through this process in order to get on with the "real purpose." But in the early stages, at least, this will be counter-productive. Take your time. Learn to relax fully, physically, and you will find that your hypnosis comes that much easier. In other words, physical relaxation is not merely a prelude to hypnosis, but it is part of the process—especially in the early stages, while you are learning. So, again, take your time, and learn to relax thoroughly.

Try, in fact, for the nearly euphoric feeling of wondering which way your feet are pointing! This probably sounds strange to you, but people who have worked on relaxation techniques know the feeling well. Your feet, legs, and stomach, your back, shoulders, and neck become *so* relaxed that you don't feel them at all. You are a brain lying there, not knowing in which direction your body extends! *That* is relaxation, and that is what you should strive for.

Don't make the mistake of trying to take shortcuts. "Long" cuts—an attention to thoroughness—will end up saving you time.

Mental Relaxation/Envisioning

Mental relaxation, begun already through the physical relaxation process, is continued by running across your mind pictures of serenity. You may imagine you are driving on a country road, lying in a field of autumn leaves, lying on an air mattress in a quiet lake, or sleeping on a cloud. The particular mental pictures you use are not important, just as long as you use pictures that suggest to you peace, comfort, and relaxation.

Let your pictures roll across your mind gently as you try to imagine them in detail—the smell of newly mown grass, perhaps, or the sound of a sailboat swishing through the water. Think of colors and smells and sounds, and any other details that help make the pictures more real to you.

Hold these mental scenes of serenity in your mind, or let them run across your mind for several minutes—then you are prepared to move to the next step.

Induction

When great baseball players are inducted into the Hall of Fame, they go through a sort of "rite of passage" ceremony. Your induction into a hypnotic trance can be thought of as that kind of passage. You are "traveling" into the depths of your own mind, and it seems to help most people to imagine a journey downward. The actual purpose of these mental images is to give your mind something on which to focus its attention so that it may begin emitting the kind of waves that are conducive to reprogramming. Naturally, you are not really taking a physical journey, but it does seem to be helpful to imagine one.

The more concrete the pictures you see on your journey, the more real and effective it will be. I personally like to begin by imagining myself entering some huge underground caverns. I like to picture a world that looks very different from anything I am accustomed to day by day. Then I imagine myself closing a huge door and locking it behind me. I walk through a medieval type of castle until I get to, of all things, an escalator.

I have never found the incongruity of the various segments of my journey to hinder the process. Knowing that the journey is an imaginary one, it doesn't seem to hurt to imagine things that don't normally go together. The important thing seems to be your mental pictures' ability to focus your attention.

I particularly like the escalator image, because on an escalator your environment gradually changes but you do not move. You are in one room and then suddenly you are in another. It goes slowly, but you do see one room disappear as another comes into view.

You can choose any group of images that help you to imagine yourself making a journey. Finally, it is often useful for you to count down as you are nearing your destination. As my escalator moves downward, I count, "10, 9, 8, 7, 6, 5, 4, 3, 2, 1—*The Inner Mind.*"

When I finish counting, I see a sign above a little room, and I enter to find something resembling an airplane cockpit. I go in and imagine that I am sitting at the controls of my own mind. I am at the center, at the place where I can change the tapes, reprogram, and record my own ideas and desires so that they can be played back when I need them.

Again, it is not crucial that you choose precisely this mental image, but you will likely find that some similar form of thought will enable you to reach the inner part of your mind that you wish to influence.

Imprinting

This is when you lay out the things you are using hypnosis for. If you have followed the first four steps, you will likely have induced a hypnotic state, an altered brain-wave frequency that will allow your statements to be recorded more deeply in your inner mind. What is important now is that you record clear, positive pictures while your mind is in this highly suggestive state.

Let me emphasize again: clear, *positive* pictures. Your mind re-members in pictures, not in words. Words are what we use to express our thoughts to others—but words do not sit in our brains and influence our actions. Pictures do. Therefore, wordy recordings do not work. Neither do negative ones. Consider nail-biting. If you get into a hypnotic state and you say, "I do not want to bite my nails," the primary picture is one of biting nails with a "not" attached, which gets lost in the shuffle because the mind has difficulty picturing a "not." If you want to stop biting your nails, it would be better to give the mind a picture of beautiful nails. Your mind can hold that picture.

The important thing, then, about the imprint phase of hypnosis is to offer the mind clear pictures of what you want. If you want to be calm and cool under pressure in a game, you wouldn't give your mind a command like "I don't want to be nervous," but instead you would give it a picture of yourself walking coolly to bat, or calmly to the free-throw line. You give it the pictures of what you want to look like in the future when a potential conflict arises. A dieter would give the mind a picture of himself or herself as slim and attractive, so when a future temptation arises, that picture comes back and enables the dieter to avoid eating because that picture has replaced the usual picture of satisfying, delicious food.

Give your mind positive mental pictures and they will influence your behavior later on in the way you desire. *This* is the delight of hypnosis. It is incredible how much easier it is to behave the way you want to when your inner mind is agreeing with you, rather than holding up some tempting, conflicting idea.

Withdrawal

This is simply the process of moving out of hypnosis, and it is easy. In fact, it is often very difficult to stay in hypnosis. The mind is not accustomed to long periods of altered brain-wave frequency, so it has the tendency, when left alone, to move back to the normal state quickly.

If you follow and complete the first five steps, it won't be long—regardless of what you do—until you are back to normal. In many cases, you will be so relaxed that you will fall asleep and this will automatically alter your brain-wave frequency. If you do not fall asleep (and it's better that you don't get into that habit, or you'll start sleeping through the first five steps as well) you can withdraw from the hypnotic state simply by making a quick upward journey, out of the caverns, back to "real" life. I usually do this in just several seconds by saying, "I will leave now, I will now leave my inner mind and move back to normal." I then picture myself walking into an elevator and watch the numbers light up as the elevator moves up five floors (while I count 1, 2, 3, 4, 5); the door opens and I walk out, open my eyes, and resume life.

As I have said, there is really nothing to the withdrawal. It is probably necessary only so you get in the habit of breaking from the hypnotic state quickly, so that your recordings have that clarity and uncomplicated look of the camera-*zip* photograph. You don't want dozens of recordings being made at random on your inner mind. So you enter, you make your few brief, forceful statements, and you leave, returning to normal.

Don't bother wondering if you are "out" of the hypnotic state. You'll be out. What you will wonder is whether you were ever "in."

Were You Ever in a Hypnotic Trance?

This is everyone's question, as I've said before. And, as I've also said, you won't feel any grand or dramatic feeling, so you will likely think that nothing has happened. But something will happen. As with sports, practice makes perfect, or at least it makes you better. The more you undergo the hypnotic process, the better your mind will be at accepting it.

You may *never* feel as though you have actually been "in," but your results will show that you have. Someday you may say, "Hypnosis didn't work, but I did solve my problem myself around the time I began experimenting with hypnosis." Indeed, it will be *you* who did it. Hypnosis is a silent, imperceptible, natural process that helps us to help ourselves.

Don't Overtest Yourself

Telling a person who is just beginning hypnosis not to test him- or herself, not to ask, "Am I in? Is it working? Is anything happening?" is like telling a little kid to stay out of a cookie jar. It is impossible for you not to wonder if something is working or happening. Your natural curiosity will force you to ask yourself these questions; but then your intelligence has to take over as well. You have to remind yourself that you are not going to hear ringing bells, experience some hallucinogenic high, or feel different from normal. Knowing this in advance, you have to be willing to give the process a chance, on faith, and just let go a little. Though you are going to be wondering and asking yourself questions, you can't second-guess experience, or you will inhibit it.

You'll be in and out constantly, without ever knowing it. You simply have to give the process a chance to work without questioning it every second. At some point you have to be willing to say to yourself, "I'll try this. What do I have to lose? At the very least, positive thoughts in a relaxed setting can't be bad," and then go from there. You have to let a bit of faith and intelligence interrupt your constant desire to question and doubt.

Taking It to the Field

Instinct Versus Decision

In sports, you want to get to the point where you're just out there doing it, not thinking about it. In tennis, for example, if you're running to a ball deciding whether to hit it down the line or cross-court, you'll likely hit the ball less effectively than if you just run and smack it one way or the other because your inner self simply took over and did it.

But you can only achieve this kind of intelligent, flowing responsiveness through practice. You do things over and over again, and your body learns to do them in the best way possible. There is no substitute for training. If you hope to hit pressure free-throws at the end of a game, you better make sure you learn to make them easily in practice, long before any real games are ever played.

You cannot hypnotize your way to self-confidence if your training does not warrant it. You cannot walk up to a free-throw line and sink two pressure shots if your "summer percentage" is only 62. You have to practice, develop the proper form and an effortless motion, and hit 90 percent in the summer, and then you'll hit those big free-throws in the games.

Remember, hypnosis is not magic. But what it *can* do is prepare you mentally to perform up to your potential. It can help you run to a tennis ball and not be paralyzed with indecision, but it can't make a cross-court winner for you in a big match if you haven't learned to make those shots consistently in practice.

Pictures of Success

When you are under hypnosis, you need to present to your mind vivid pictures of yourself succeeding in the circumstances you are currently worried about. If your problem in sports, for example, is nervousness, get into a practice game with a group of little kids—players you are obviously better than—and feel what it is like to perform with confidence against them. Then, during hypnosis, feed that same picture to your mind, but substitute bigger, better players around you. Picture yourself doing your thing with confidence and skill against anyone, because you can. And you deserve to have that kind of confidence, if you have raised your skill level to be able to perform at that level.

Remember, feed your brain positive, clear, vivid pictures of yourself in successful situations—dribbling deftly past a defender, hitting a backhand passing shot from the deep corner, standing tall and calm as you look over the secondary to find your receiver, or stroking in a thirty-foot putt for a birdie. Whatever you are trying to accomplish, feed your brain pictures of those accomplishments and then *practice and train* so you are indeed capable of doing those things.

Success is a two-way street, mental and physical, and you have to be attentive to both areas in order to achieve the satisfaction and the goals that you set for yourself.

When the Big Moment Arrives

So, you have been hypnotized, you have created the right circumstances, and you have listened to your cassette dozens of times—every day for the first few weeks and now several times a week—but what now? You still have to hit the ball or make the free-throw.

You know what? You can.

At first, you may feel that old nervous failure-feeling coming back, and you may begin to think, "What was I doing all that time? Here I am, it's just me, and all those old feelings are here again." At first. But then something wonderful will happen. Something inside you, coming from those tapes you put in there, will start saying, "Hold everything, wait a minute, *this ain't so baaad.*"

In the movie *Rocky III,* Clubber Lang (Mr. T) was giving Rocky a beating, and Rocky was cowering. Rocky had admitted earlier that he was afraid, and now, despite his long training, the fear had returned—until suddenly something clicked. It was that inner voice saying, "Wait a minute, hold everything." And at that point, Rocky let go. He quit worrying about being hit; he let go of his fear. In fact, he *let* his opponent hit him, because he finally realized that he had let his opponent become larger-than-life. He had let Clubber Lang become fear itself. The man had become unrealistic in Rocky's mind, and suddenly Rocky realized it. Clubber Lang was not so "bad" after all. He wasn't so great. Rocky had just let fear take hold. But because of his training, his mind was able to reassert itself and he realized that he had the ability to get the job done.

Rocky III is only a movie, but it contains some very astute sports psychology. Sometimes you have to just let go before you realize that you can do it. But it takes training and effort to get to that point. You can't expect your inner voice to tell you the right things if you haven't trained it to do so.

If you walk up to a free-throw line and begin to get those old nervous feelings—"Oh no, here I go again; I always choke in these circumstances"—you will find they will suddenly leave you as fast as they came, *if* you have taken time to train your inner mind to prepare for this. Then the "here I go again" will suddenly vanish, because you aren't trying desperately to push it away. Instead you're thinking, "Yes, I know that feeling, I know it is a pressure situation, but I can handle it. I can be calm. I have trained for this moment." You won't have to concentrate to keep these feelings in your head, because you took the time to put them there.

And what an exhilarating feeling you are going to have when you suddenly begin to feel that, indeed, *this ain't so bad!*

It's like walking up to a podium to make a speech. If you clench your fists in order to keep your hands from shaking with nervousness, you will only shake more. But if you walk up there and nod to the audience, hold out your arms and say, "My, I'm nervous. You must be very important people," then you can shake and laugh and enjoy the moment. Don't fight it. So here's pressure. Big deal. You *should* be somewhat nervous. You would be crazy and inhuman if you weren't. But now you can handle it. You can enjoy it. Because it ain't so bad.

Evaluating Your Program and Yourself

A Realistic Look

One of the things that all athletes have to learn to do is to look at themselves realistically and evaluate where they are going and what they are doing. If you are five feet eight inches tall and slow, you really can't expect to be an NBA basketball player someday, and it is foolish for you to feel frustrated because your game is not up to NBA standards.

We all need to look at ourselves, in general, and as a performer in particular situations, in order to set realistic goals and expectations. It doesn't do you any good to set goals far above your ability, nor does it help your mental health to live your life feeling like a failure because you didn't accomplish this or that dream.

I meet many athletes who want tips on how to become Atlantic Coast Conference basketball players, because the ACC is very popular in the southeast and I once played ACC basketball. Most of these athletes will one day be disillusioned with the sport because they failed to make the ACC. But they shouldn't be disillusioned, because they aren't even vaguely realistic about what they want or how they are going to get it. Even parents ask, "Do you think my son can make it? He's growing and getting stronger, and he takes that basketball with him out in the driveway every day after school."

What the parent and the kid don't realize is that kids destined to play in the ACC aren't shooting up some lazy shots in the driveway every day after school during the fall. They are practicing year-round, every day for five or six hours, and they are working furiously to improve. They are shooting hundreds of shots and charting each one; they are like gunslingers, always out looking for a game, always meeting new opponents and trying to figure out new ways of doing things so they won't keep getting beat by the same techniques. The kid shooting in his suburban driveway in the fall is in no way preparing for playing in the ACC. He is living in a dream world.

Write It Down

One of the best ways to check yourself and what you are doing is to write down your circumstances. Take the time to say, "This is what I want, this is what will make me happy, and this is what I am willing to do to get it." If you are only willing to spend a couple of hours in your driveway shooting in the fall, even you will probably realize that you are not being realistic when you see it written down on paper.

Write down what you want and how you are preparing, and see if it seems realistic to you. Then show it to your parents, or to a friend. And finally, try to consult someone who should know something about the subject—a coach if your goal is sports-related, or the drama teacher if your goal is to act.

It is foolish to spend your life feeling like a failure if you simply had no realistic chance to succeed with your approach.

Failure

I would like to finish with this last word, because I think it is especially important, in a book on success, to look its opposite squarely in the eye. What is failure? Failure means you didn't do what you set out to do. Okay. How bad is that? You can't win every game you ever play, you can't sink every putt, or ace every serve. No one can.

In other words, sometimes failure is merely *the best you possibly could have done under the circumstances.* Sometimes, despite a realistic plan and a diligent, prolonged effort, you still will not succeed. Take Mary Decker for example. She trained long and hard, she overcame all sorts of physical ailments and the bitterness of the 1980

Olympic boycott, in order to go to the 1984 Olympic Games at the peak of her abilities, prepared to win the gold medal. But despite all that, she was tripped during her big race and fell off the track, and was carried off the field in tears.

She did her best, and she lost. Sometimes that happens in life. You cannot control the outcome of your efforts. You can only control the process. You can be sure that your efforts are intelligent ones, that you are getting the most from yourself, and that you are learning how to compete—yet you must learn to take the setbacks along with the triumphs.

No one gets everything he or she wants. You win some, you lose some. We all know that. And we all know all the famous sports clichés—"It's not whether you win or lose, but how you play the game."

Sometimes I think that a cliché like that is a rationalization for people who have prepared poorly and lost often. Good athletes don't take a lot of solace in how they played the game. They play to win, and they are sorry, dejected, and disappointed when they lose. But they do know, ultimately, that there are no guarantees. The only thing that makes the whole experience make sense is that you learn to play hard and to compete intelligently and furiously *to the very best of your ability*. If you lose, then and only then do you say, "I guess it just wasn't meant to be."

Some things are not meant to be. They just aren't going to happen. But don't use that as a rationalization until you have done everything in your power to make them happen. Once you have done that, if you fail, then you really won't feel as bad as you thought you would.

Failure isn't as bad as it once may have seemed to the person who has truly given his or her very best—and *knows* it.